Basic ESL Workbook

The companion book to Basic ESL *Online*:
www.basicesl.com

LEVEL 2

C. Sesma, M. A.
ESL and Spanish Teacher

Bilingual Dictionaries, Inc.

Basic ESL® Workbook: Level 2
English as a Second Language

Publisher:
Bilingual Dictionaries, Inc.
P.O.Box 1154
Murrieta, CA 92564
Website: www.bilingualdictionaries.com
Email: support@bilingualdictionaries.com

Content by C. Sesma, M.A.
English and Spanish Teacher

Design by John Garcia

ISBN13: 978-0-933146-24-2
ISBN: 0-933146-24-8

The **Basic ESL® Workbooks** are the companion books to **Basic ESL® Online.**
Basic ESL Online provides:
> Online English Learning
> Audio Pronunciation of English
> Native Language Support

For **information** and **registration** to Basic ESL® Online please visit the the Basic ESL® website:
Website: www.BasicESL.com
Email: info@basicesl.com

Prologue

The **Basic ESL Workbook** is the companion book to **Basic ESL Online (www.basicesl.com)**. Except for the English pronunciations and native language translations that are provided online, this book follows the online course content with some adjustments required by the book format. Since written grammatical exercises cannot be provided online, this book has added an extra section at the end of each lesson. The written exercises section provides the ability to test the student's progress and knowledge of the English language structure. In order for the student to get the best of Basic ESL, it is very important to be familiar with the goals and learning methods of the online lessons found at www.basicesl.com.

The **main goal** of Basic ESL Online is to develop the oral skills of communication rather than trying to memorize grammatical rules. The first oral skill of communication is **to be able to understand the spoken English**. This is accomplished by continuous listening to the oral exercises, stories, dialogs and conversations. The second and most important oral skill of communication is **to be able to ask and answer questions.**

To accomplish these goals, Basic ESL offers simple and effective learning methods that will help the student succeed in learning English as a Second Language:

1. The gradual, step by step approach of learning the English language. Each lesson is built on the knowledge of the previous lessons, in addition to the new content for that lesson.

2. The Lesson Sections (A-H): the vocabulary study, the sentence structure, the listening exercises, the conversation exercises and the presentation of common phrases used by native English speakers.

3. The English Pronunciation. At Basic ESL Online, the students are in control of the English pronunciation by allowing them to listen and repeat all the words and sentences as many times as needed.

4. The Translations. The translation of the English vocabulary and sentence structures into the native language of the student will speed up the process of learning English. The translations are also a great tool for self-study at home or at the local library.

5. The Explanation of Grammatical Concepts. Students who want to learn the mechanics of the language will find grammar concepts explained in their native language. By clicking on the **information button** ℹ at Basic ESL Online, students can view the translated grammar concepts that go along with the lesson.

The Basic ESL Workbook works together with Basic ESL Online (www.basicesl.com) to give English language learners a simple and effective way to learn English as a second language. Basic ESL Online provides the audio English pronunciation for the different lesson sections as well as the written native language translations. We strongly recommend all Basic ESL students to register for Basic ESL Online at www.basicesl.com.

Recommendation to the Student

In order to obtain the best results from the use of this Basic ESL Workbook, we recommend the student becomes a member of **Basic ESL Online** at:

www.basicesl.com

Here the student will find the audio English pronunciations, the native language translation support of the vocabulary and the sentence structures, plus the grammar explanations in the language of the student.

Contents

Chapter 1
Meals

Lesson 1:   Breakfast - Lunch
Lesson 2:   Dinner - Supper
Lesson 3:   Home Cooking

What to do in each section of every lesson...

A - Vocabulary Study

Section A includes the vocabulary that will be used throughout the lesson. Learning new vocabulary is basic to learning a new language.

Read the vocabulary several times.
If you are on Basic ESL Online:
Listen to the **English audio pronunciation**.
View the **native language translations** of the vocabulary.

Listen and read the vocabulary until you can understand the vocabulary without looking at the words.

B - Sentence Structure

Section B teaches students basic English sentences using the vocabulary in section A.

Read and **study** the sentences.
If you are on Basic ESL Online:
Listen to the **English audio pronunciation**.
View the **native language translations** of the sentences.
View the **grammar concepts** by clicking on the **information button** .

Repeat the sentences as many times as needed. Continue to the next section once you can **understand** the sentences without looking at them.

C - Listening Exercises

Read the story or dialog several times.
If you are on Basic ESL Online, **listen** to the story or dialog while reading it several times.

Once you are familiar with the story or dialog, try to see if you can **understand** it by only listening without reading.

D - Conversation Exercises

Read the conversation dialogs several times.
If you are on Basic ESL Online, **listen** to the dialogs until you can understand them without looking at them.

Finally, try to **speak** the conversation dialogs by only looking at the pictures and key words.

E - Common Phrases

Many of the **common phrases** that are presented in this section are frequently used by the native English speakers in their everyday life.

Read the common phrases several times.
If you are on Basic ESL Online, **listen** to the common phrases while reading. **Listen** as many times as needed until you can understand the common phrases without looking at the sentences.

H - Written Exercises

The written exercises provide an opportunity to test what you learned in the lesson. You can never be sure of knowing something unless you can put it in writing.

You can check your answers by going to the **Answer Key Section** in the back of the workbook.

For information regarding **Basic ESL Online,** please visit **www.basicesl.com**.
Audio Pronunciaton of English & Native Language Translations.

Lesson #1

Breakfast & Lunch

Index

Audio & Translations

English Audio available online for sections A-E.

Translations in various Languages available online for Sections A, B, and E.

www.BasicESL.com

1. butter

2. toast

3. bacon

4. eggs

5. coffee

6. sausage

7. tea

8. sugar

9. hamburger

10. pizza

11. hotdog

12. soup

13. salad

14. french fries

15. sandwich

16. salad dressing

17. cereal

18. pancake

19. breakfast

20. lunch

21. orange juice

Other Vocabulary

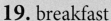

1.	n	pantry	10.	v	complain
2.	n	place	11.	v	order
3.	adj	full	12.	v	place
4.	adj	jealous	13.	adv	always
5.	adj	selfish	14.	adv	never
6.	adj	upset	15.	adv	frequently
7.	v	break	16.	pro	none
8.	v	burn	17.	con	but
9.	v	carry	18.	pre	instead

For the audio pronunciations and written translations of **Sections A and B,** please go to:

www.basicesl.com

Looking for Bilingual Dictionaries?
You can find a large selection at:

www.bilingualdictionaries.com

B1. Phrase "there is, there are": Statements

Aff	**There is** some fruit.
Neg	**There isn't** any fruit.
Neg	**There is no** fruit.
Aff	**There are** some eggs.
Neg	**There aren't** any eggs.
Neg	**There are no** eggs.
Aff	**There is** some water.
Neg	**There isn't** any water.
Neg	**There is no** water.

B1 - B2

"There is" or *"there are"* is a common phrase used to indicate existence. We use *"there is"* with a singular subject. *"There are"* is used with a plural subject.

B2. Phrase "there is, there are: Statements

Aff	**There are** many pies there.
Neg	**There aren't** any pies there.
Neg	**There are no** pies there.
Aff	Today **there is** soup.
Neg	Today **there isn't** any soup.
Neg	Today **there is no** soup.
Aff	**There is** tea for breakfast.
Neg	**There isn't** any tea for lunch.
Neg	**There is no** tea for lunch

B3. Phrase "there is, there are": Questions (Q)

	There is bacon for breakfast.
Q	**Is there** bacon for breakfast?
	There is some soup for lunch.
Q	**Is there** any soup for lunch?
	There are sandwiches for lunch.
Q	**Are there** sandwiches for lunch?
	There are some prunes for breakfast.
Q	**Are there** any prunes for breakfast?

B4. Phrase "there is, there are": Short Answers

Is there any hot coffee?
Yes, **there is** some.
Yes, **there is**.

Are there any french fries?
No, there aren't any.
No, there aren't.

Is there any bacon for lunch?
No, there isn't any.
No, there isn't.

B4 - B5

Short answers are formed by only repeating the verb used in the question.

B5. Phrase "there is, there are": Short Answers

Are there any eggs for lunch?
Yes, there are some.
Yes, there are.

Are there any sandwiches today?
No, there aren't any.
No, there aren't.

Is there any butter?
Yes, there is some.
Yes, there is.

B6. Adverbs: "when" and "while"

When do you read the newspaper?
I read the newspaper **while** I eat.

When do you listen to music?
I listen to music **while** I run.

When do you clean the house?
I do it **while** the baby sleeps.

When does your mom rest?
She rests **while** I am at school.

C1. Read and Listen to the story.

My three sisters eat two meals at home. Before going to school they eat a light breakfast: a glass of orange juice and a bowl of cereal. Our parents have a cup of coffee and a piece of toast with marmalade. When there is no milk they drink water.

Today there is no juice in the refrigerator. There are only two bottles of milk. There are no boxes of cereals in the pantry. Also, there is no jar of marmalade. This is why my sisters are eating ham and eggs today. Instead of a light breakfast, they are having a full breakfast.

C2. Read and Listen to the story.

Pat **enjoys** art and music. She also **learns** geography with her teacher Mrs. Brown. Pat **loves** her teacher. The name of her teacher **is** Ann. She **is** from Mexico. She **is** twenty-three years old and she **has** a big family.

Pat **is** smart. Her writing **is** very good. She also **speaks** good English. Besides English, she **learns** Spanish and French at school. She **does not speak** French well. Her favorite subjects **are** spelling and foreign languages. She **likes** art also. She **does not like** music.

She **has** good grades in history and math. She **does not have** good grades in French. Her friend Lucy **likes** social studies and sports. Her coach Carol **is** her favorite teacher.

D1. you

Do you want butter?
I like butter for breakfast.
I don't like butter for lunch.

Is there any butter today?
There is butter only for breakfast.
There is no butter for lunch.

D2. brother

Does your brother want eggs?
He wants eggs for breakfast.
He doesn't like eggs for lunch.

Are there any eggs today?
There are eggs only for breakfast.
There are no eggs for lunch.

D3. sister

Does your sister want toast?
She wants toast for breakfast.
She doesn't want toast for lunch.

Is there any toast today?
There is toast only for breakfast.
There is no toast for lunch.

D4. uncles

Do your uncles like coffee?
They want coffee for breakfast.
They don't want coffee for lunch.

Is there any coffee today?
There is coffee only for breakfast.
There is no coffee for lunch.

Asking permission

1. May I go to the bathroom?
2. *Yes, it is down the hall.*
3. May I make a phone call?
4. *No, not now.*
5. May I sit down here?
6. *Yes, you may.*
7. May I ask you a question?
8. *Go ahead.*
9. May I go home now?
10. *Wait ten more minutes.*

For the English audio pronunciations and written native language translations of **section E,** please go to:

www.basicesl.com

May I make a phone call?

May I ask a question?

End of the **oral exercises** for lesson 1.
You can find additional exercises in sections D, F & G at Basic ESL Online.

Please continue with the **written exercises** for this lesson in **section H.**

Lesson

1

H1. Complete with *there is* or *there are*.

1. *There is* _____ chocolate in the pantry.

2. _____ some eggs for breakfast.

3. _____ fish for lunch.

4. _____ sausages in the store.

5. _____ soup for the grandparents.

6. _____ some sandwiches today.

7. _____ salad for lunch.

8. _____ pineapples in the kitchen.

9. _____ hot dogs in the coffee shop.

10. _____ pizza today for lunch.

11. _____ also French fries.

12. _____ butter in the refrigerator.

13. _____ toast with marmalade for breakfast.

H2. Make questions.

1. There is some chocolate. *Is there* any chocolate?
2. There are some peaches. _____
3. There is some bacon today. _____
4. There are fried eggs. _____
5. There is soup for lunch. _____
6. There are some apples. _____
7. There is salad today. _____
8. There is some coffee. _____
9. There are sausages for lunch. _____
10. There are all kinds of tea. _____

H3. Answer the questions with short answers.

1. Is there any coffee today? *Yes, there is some.*
   No, there isn't any.
2. Are there any knives in the drawer? _____
3. Are there any grapes for lunch? _____
4. Is there any bread for breakfast? _____
5. Are there any children at home? _____

H4. Make the sentences negative.

1. There is some chocolate.

   *There is **no** chocolate.*

   *There **isn't** any chocolate.*

2. There are some peaches.

3. There is some bacon today.

4. There are fried eggs.

5. There is soup for lunch.

6. There are some apples.

7. There is salad today.

8. There is some coffee.

9. There are sausages for lunch.

H5. Follow the example.

1.   breakfast

fruit

Is there any fruit for breakfast?
Yes, there is some fruit for breakfast.
Is there any fruit for lunch?
No, there is no fruit for lunch.

2.   lunch

sweets

_____
_____
_____
_____

3.   breakfast

fish

_____
_____
_____
_____

4.   lunch

soup

_____
_____
_____
_____

5.   breakfast

pies

_____
_____
_____
_____

Lesson #2

Dinner & Supper

Index

Audio & Translations

 English Audio available online for sections A-E.

 Translations in various Languages available online for Sections A, B, and E.

www.BasicESL.com

A - Picture Vocabulary  🎧 2-2

1. fish

2. meat

3. lamb

4. turkey

5. steak

6. roast beef

7. oil and vinegar

8. salt

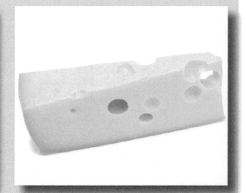

9. cheese

10. wine

11. honey

12. pepper

13. sweets

14. biscuit

15. chocolate

16. pie

17. spaghetti

18. ice cream

19. cake   **20.** dessert   **21.** nuts

Other Vocabulary

1.	n	cork	**10.**	v	melt
2.	n	course	**11.**	v	pour
3.	n	shrimp	**12.**	v	reject
4.	n	taste	**13.**	v	request
5.	n	veal	**14.**	v	serve
6.	adj	canned	**15.**	v	spoil
7.	adj	homemade	**16.**	v	wrap
8.	adj	hungry	**17.**	adv	however
9.	adj	thirsty	**18.**	pre	before

For the audio pronunciations and written translations of **Sections A and B,** please go to:

www.basicesl.com

Looking for Bilingual Dictionaries?
You can find a large selection at:

www.bilingualdictionaries.com

B1. Count nouns and Non-Count nouns

i

Count nouns:	Non-count nouns:
cork	sugar
pie	wine
egg	coffee
sandwich	soup
cookie	water
potato	juice
fig	honey
apple	oil

B1

Count nouns are those that can be counted.

Non-count nouns are those that cannot be counted.

B2. Quantity Adjectives: Count and Non-Count nouns

Count nouns

Aff	I want **lots of** glasses.
Aff	I want **many** glasses.
Aff	I want **a few** glasses.
Neg	I don't want **many** glasses.

Non-count nouns

Aff	I need **a lot of** milk.
Aff	I need **a little** milk.
Neg	I don't need **much** milk.

B2

Quantity adjectives are those that indicate an amount of something or a number of people or objects.

The former are used with count nouns. The latter are used with non-count nouns.

B3. Question Words: Count Nouns: "how many"

i

How many figs does she eat?
She eats **lots of** figs.

How many eggs do you cook?
I cook **many** eggs.

How many sausages are they buying?
They are buying **plenty of** sausages.

How many steaks do you need?
I need **a few** steaks.

B3

"How many" is used with **count nouns** to obtain information about the **number** of people or things.

"Plenty" is used with count and non-count nouns.

B4. Question Words: Non-Count Nouns: "how much"

B4

How much soup do you want?
I want **a lot of** soup.

How much salt does she use?
She uses a **small** amount.

How much water do they drink?
They drink **plenty of** water.

How much vinegar do we have?
We still have **a little** vinegar.

"How much" is used with *non-count nouns* in questions to obtain information about the **quantity** or the **amount**.

B5. Comparative Adjectives: "fewer, less"

B5

How many people are there?
There were **fewer** people.
They have **less** interest now.

How many dollars do you have?
I have **fewer** dollars.
I have **less** money now.

How many times do you go there?
I go there **fewer** times.
I have **less** time to go there.

"Fewer" is used with count nouns.

"Less" is used with non-count nouns.

B6. Progressive Form: Negative Sentences

B6 (Review)

    I usually **eat** potatoes.
PF   Today I **am not eating** potatoes.

You usually **eat** onions.
PF   Today you **are not eating** onions.

Ann usually **eats** carrots.
PF   Today she **is not eating** carrots.

We usually **eat** lettuce.
PF   Today we **are not eating** lettuce.

C1. Read and Listen to the Story.

Mrs. Gray prepares dinner every day. She usually cooks beef or turkey for dinner. There is plenty of beef and chicken in the freezer, but there is not much fish. The children don't care much for fish.

They start dinner with a bowl of soup. They like homemade soup, especially chicken soup. They hate canned soup. After eating the soup, Mrs. Gray serves the main course. This course consists of meat or fish with potatoes, rice or vegetables.

There is always some dessert after dinner. It consists of a piece of cake, a few cookies or a lot of ice cream.

C2. Read and Listen to the dialog.

Who prepares dinner?
Mrs Gray does.

What does she cook for dinner?
She usually cooks meat.

Does she cook fish?
She rarely cooks fish.

Why doesn't she cook fish?
The children don't care for fish.

Do they like soup?
Yes, they are crazy about soup.

What kind of soup do they like?
They like homemade soup.

Does Mrs. Gray serve vegetables?
Yes, she does.

What kind of vegetables?
They eat all kinds.

Which are their favorite vegetables?
Carrots and lettuce.

What do they eat for dessert?
Thy eat cake with ice-cream.

D1. you / have / salt

Do you have any sugar or salt?
I have both.
I have sugar and salt.

How much do you have?
I have a lot of sugar.
I do not have much salt.

D2. she / want / pies

Does she want any cakes or pies?
Yes, she wants both.
She wants cakes and pies.

How many does she want?
She wants lots of cakes.
She does not want many pies.

D3. they / need / ice cream

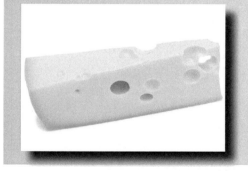

Do they need any cheese or ice cream?
Yes, they need both.
They need cheese and ice cream.

How much do they need?
They need a lot of cheese.
They don't need much ice cream.

D4. Ray / buy / pears

Does Ray buy apples or pears?
Yes, he buys both.
He buys apples and pears.

How many does he buy?
He buys lots of apples.
He does not buy many pears.

Useful Phrases

1. Hi, Mary. You look great.
2. *Thanks for the compliment.*
3. How is it going?
4. *Fine, except for Julian.*
5. Is he your friend?
6. *No way.*
7. What's wrong with him?
8. *I can't stand him. He drives me crazy.*
9. Why don't you get rid of him?
10. *It is not so easy.*

For the English audio pronunciations and written native language translations of **section E,** please go to:

www.basicesl.com

How is it going?

Hi, Mary. You look great.

End of the **oral exercises** for lesson 2.
You can find additional exercises in sections D, F & G at Basic ESL Online.

Please continue with the **written exercises** for this lesson in **section H.**

Lesson

2

H1. Mark the type of noun.

	Count	Non-count			Count	Non-count
1. bed	X	_____	8. loaf		_____	_____
2. bottle	_____	_____	9. meat		_____	_____
3. bowl	_____	_____	10. pantry		_____	_____
4. biscuits	_____	_____	11. pie		_____	_____
5. butter	_____	_____	12. pillow		_____	_____
6. cake	_____	_____	13. sugar		_____	_____
7. can	_____	_____	14. salt		_____	_____

H2. Complete with the question words *how much* **or** *how many*.

1.	*How many*	kinds of salad are there?
2.	_____	bottles of beer do they drink?
3.	_____	oil do you use for cooking?
4.	_____	salt does mom put in the soup?
5.	_____	dishes is she preparing in the kitchen?
6.	_____	wine does she drink?
7.	_____	milk do you want in your coffee?
8.	_____	pineapples are there in the kitchen?

H3. Mark the correct quantity adjective(s) used with the count noun.

	a few	lots of	many	
1. **I have**	X	X	X	peaches.
I don't have	_____	_____	X	apricots.
2. I eat	_____	_____	_____	pies.
I don't eat	_____	_____	_____	cakes.
3. She needs	_____	_____	_____	vegetables.
She doesn't need	_____	_____	_____	lemons.
4. Tom buys	_____	_____	_____	cherries.
Tom doesn't buy	_____	_____	_____	grapes.
5. They order	_____	_____	_____	sandwiches.
They don't order	_____	_____	_____	hamburgers.

H4. Mark the correct quantity adjective(s) used with the non-count nouns.

	a little	a lot of	much	
1. I have	X	X	_____	butter.
I **don't** have	_____	_____	X	honey.
2. I eat	_____	_____	_____	fish.
I **don't** eat	_____	_____	_____	meat.
3. She needs	_____	_____	_____	sauce.
She **doesn't** need	_____	_____	_____	salt.
4. Tom buys	_____	_____	_____	sugar.
Tom **doesn't** buy	_____	_____	_____	wine.
5. They order	_____	_____	_____	coffee.
They **don't** order	_____	_____	_____	milk.

H5. Complete with *many, much, a lot of, lots of, a little, a few*.

1. We don't carry   ***many*** _____ sandwiches.
2. We carry _____ ice-cream.

3. Henry breaks _____ glasses.
4. He doesn't break _____ plates.

5. She puts _____ salt in the soup.
6. She doesn't put _____ salt on the fish.

7. I don't chop _____ onions.
8. I chop _____ potatoes.

9. They don't eat _____ ham.
10. They eat _____ cheese.

11. Sara cooks a _____ chicken.
12. She doesn't cook _____ steaks.

13. I pour _____ wine.
14. I don't pour _____ beer.

15. He peels _____ oranges.
16. He doesn't peel _____ tangerines.

H6. Follow the example.

1.   I / vegetables

fruit

*I have **a lot** of fruit.*
*I don't have **many** vegetables.*
*I like fruit **a lot**.*
*I don't like vegetables **much**.*

2.   Ryan / cheese

sweets

_____

_____

_____

3.   we / cookies

ice-cream

_____

_____

_____

4.   parents / coffee

bottles of wine

_____

_____

_____

5.   you / eggs

honey

_____

_____

_____

Lesson #3

Home Cooking

Index

Audio & Translations

 English Audio available online for sections A-E.

 Translations in various Languages available online for Sections A, B, and E.

www.BasicESL.com

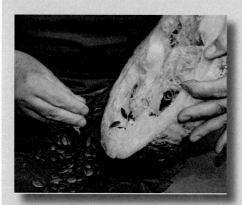

1. remove (*the seeds*)

2. split (*a melon*)

3. cut (*a banana*)

4. peel (*an orange*)

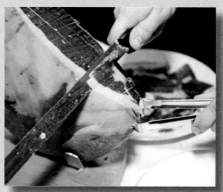

5. trim (*the fat*)

6. sprinkle (*with salt*)

7. wash (*the fruit*)

8. chop (*an onion*)

9. drain (*the water*)

10. boil (*the soup*)

11. roast (*the meat*)

12. fry (*the beef*)

13. stir (*the coffee*)

14. bake (*the pie*)

15. toast (*the bread*)

16. mix (*the fruit*)

17. blend (*the juice*)

18. grind (*the pepper*)

19. to heat

20. to grill

21. to freeze

Other Vocabulary

1.	n	piece	**10.**	v	choose
2.	n	plenty	**11.**	v	bless
3.	n	seed	**12.**	v	go
4.	n	fat	**13.**	v	prepare
5.	v	cry	**14.**	v	taste
6.	v	do	**15.**	v	say
7.	v	chill	**16.**	v	simmer
8.	v	fix	**17.**	adv	together
9.	v	fly	**18.**	pre	for

For the audio pronunciations and written translations of **Sections A and B,** please go to:

www.basicesl.com

B1. Verbs: Present Tense: 3rd Person Singular

ⓘ

to melt	I **melt** the cheese. He **melts** the butter.
to pour	You **pour** the water. She **pours** the wine.
to taste	They **taste** the food. John **tastes** the salad.
to order	We **order** the bread. Sara **orders** the dessert.

B1

As a rule the present tense verb form for the 3rd person singular ("he, she, it or a noun singular") is formed by adding an "-s" to the basic form of the verb. Some verbs add different endings.

B2. Verbs ending in "h, s, x, z, ch, sh"

ⓘ

to finish	I fini**sh** the book. He finish**es** the meal.
to catch	You cat**ch** colds. She catch**es** the ball.
to mix	We mi**x** the fruit. Mom mix**es** the vegetables.
to wash	The boys wa**sh** the floors. The girl wash**es** the windows.

B2 - B3

Verbs ending in "h, s, x, z, ch, sh," and some verbs ending in "o", add "-es" in order to form 3rd person singular in the present tense.

B3. Verbs ending in "h, s, x, z, ch, sh"

relax	We rela**x** at the pool. She relax**es** at the beach.
wish	You wi**sh** to stay at school. He wish**es** to leave school.
brush	I bru**sh** my hair once a day She brush**es** her hair often.
reach	I rea**ch** London in the morning. Tom reach**es** Paris at noon.

B4. Verbs ending in "-y"

to cry	I cry when it hurts. Mary cr**ies** at night.	
to study	You study math. Alex stud**ies** music.	
to play	We play at home. Alex play**s** at the school.	
to enjoy	They enjoy the food. Tony enjoy**s** the sports.	

B4

For verbs ending in "-y" preceded by a consonant, change the "-y" to "-ies" in order to form the 3rd person singular in the present tense.

B5. Verbs: 3rd Person Singular

Is the soup delicious?
Yes, it is very delicious.
Fred **enjoys** the soup often.

Are the onions nutritious?
Yes, they are very nutritious.
My dad **fries** onions often.

Is the watermelon refreshing?
Yes, it is very refreshing.
My son **finishes** a watermelon fast.

B6. Number of Times

Pat studies **once** a day.
She works **twice** a week.
She plays ten **times** a month.

She punishes the children often.
How many **times** does she do it?
She punishes Joe **many times.**
She punishes Jane **a few times**.
At no time she punishes you.

C1. Read and Listen to the story.

Every day my **mom prepares** the main meal. **She starts** with the soup. **She makes** her favorite pea soup. **She washes** the peas and **boils** the soup on the stove.

While the soup is boiling, **she prepares** the main course of meat with onions. **She trims** the fat from the meat and **sprinkles** the meat with a little salt. **She chops** an onion and **fries** the meat with onions.

For dessert **she prepares** a fruit salad. **She splits** a melon, **peels** an orange and **cuts** a banana. Finally, **she mixes** the orange, the melon and the banana together.

C2. Read and Listen to the story.

My closet is full of clothes. I don't need many of these clothes. I have several shirts and pants, one suit with an extra coat, two jackets and an overcoat. I hang all these clothes in the closet.

I keep small clothes in the drawers of the dresser. I use the drawers for my socks, ties, sweaters, T-shirts and belts.

My sister has a closet that is also full with clothes: skirts, blouses, a robe, all kinds of dresses and scarves. She wears different clothes every day.

D1. you / cut / refreshing

What are you doing now?
I am cutting a watermelon.

Do you cut a watermelon every day?
Yes, I cut a watermelon every day.

Why do you do that?
Because watermelons are refreshing.

D2. Mom / cook / delicious

What is Mom doing now?
She is cooking soup.

Does she cook soup every day?
Yes, she cooks soup every day.

Why does she do that?
Because soup is delicious.

D3. Dad / fry / very good

What is Dad doing now?
He is frying meat.

Does he fry meat every day?
Yes, he fries meat every day.

Why does he do that?
Because meat is very good.

D4. sisters / chop / very healthy

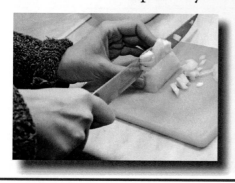

What are your sisters doing now?
They are chopping onions.

Do they chop onions every day?
Yes, they chop onions every day.

Why do they do that?
Because onions are very healthy.

In the kitchen

1. *What does Mom do in the kitchen?*
2. She chops the onions.
3. She bakes the bread.
4. She fries the chicken.
5. She mixes the salad.
6. She stirs the soup.
7. She heats the dishes.
8. She slices the cheese.
9. She roasts the meat.
10. She broils the steaks.

For the English audio pronunciations and written native language translations of **section E**, please go to:

www.basicesl.com

She stirs the soup.

She roasts the meat.

End of the **oral exercises** for lesson 3.
You can find additional exercises in sections D, F & G at Basic ESL Online.

Please continue with the **written exercises** for this lesson in **section H.**

H1. Write the correct form of the verb for the subject *he* or *she*.

he...   *she...*

1.	pour	*pours*	8.	catch	*catches*
2.	cry	_____	9.	try	_____
3.	stir	_____	10.	finish	_____
4.	study	_____	11.	watch	_____
5.	carry	_____	12.	brush	_____
6.	multiply	_____	13.	need	_____
7.	fix	_____	14.	fly	_____

H2. Change the subject to *Tom*.

1. **You** blend the juices.   *Tom blends the juices.*

2. My parents enjoy the wine.   _____

3. I mix the fruits.   _____

4. They bake pies.   _____

5. We fry the chicken.   _____

6. I play at school.   _____

7. They do homework.   _____

H3. Make the sentences negative.

1.	Tom uses a lot of sugar	*He does not use much* _____	salt.
2.	Sam drinks a lot of milk.	_____	coffee.
3.	They eat lots of cookies.	_____	fruit.
4.	There is a lot of salad.	_____	meat.
5.	We buy many bags of rice.	_____	candy.
6.	She needs lots of shrimps.	_____	sweets.
7.	I want some oil.	_____	wine.
8.	He cuts lots of potatoes.	_____	onions.
9.	Ann bakes many cakes.	_____	pies.
10.	Sara washes glasses.	_____	plates.

H4. Make the sentences plural.

1. **He** likes the meat **sausage**.   *They like the meat sausages.*
2. There is no fruit **juice**.
3. Where's the **pie**?
4. That's a big **potato**.
5. Where does **she** keep the **fork**?
6. **I** like the strawberry **cake**.
7. **You** don't like **soup**.
8. **She** pours the **wine**.
9. The **man** wraps the **sandwich**.
10. The **woman** melts the **cheese**.

H5. Re-write the story changing *my sisters* for *my mom*.

Every day **my sisters prepare** the main meal. **They start** with the soup. **They make** their favorite pea soup. **They wash** the peas in a saucepan, **drain** the water and **add** clean water. Then **they boil** the soup on the stove.

While the soup is boiling, **they prepare** the main course of meat with onions. **They trim** the fat from the meat and **sprinkle** the meat with a little salt. **They chop** an onion and **fry** the meat with onions.

For dessert **they prepare** a fruit salad. **They split** a melon and **remove** the seeds. Then **they peel** an orange and **mix** the orange with the melon.

*Every day **my mom*** _____

_____

_____

_____

_____

_____

_____

_____

_____

_____

_____

_____

_____

_____

_____

_____

_____

_____

_____

H6. Select the correct answer.

1. I spread _____ on the toast.	corn	toast	jam	cereal
2. An item without fat.	cabbage	steak	sandwich	Ice-cream
3. _____ is not a dessert.	cake	fish	pie	fruit
4. We make cheese from _____ .	custard	eggs	milk	cheese
5. A main dish.	bacon	soup	salad	spaghetti
6. We melt _____ on the pan.	cake	salt	butter	beer

H7. Multiple choice.

1. We need _____ oil.   many, much, **a lot of**

2. There isn't _____ sugar at the store.   many, much, a lot of

3. I don't drink _____ wine.   many, much, a lot of

4. I drink _____ bottles of beer.   many, much, a lot of

5. How _____ pens do you need.   many, much, a lot of

6. My sister doesn't _____ breakfast.   eating, eat, eats

7. She a big dinner. _____   eating, eat, eats

8. Today she isn't _____ much fish.   eating, eat, eats

9. Tony is _____ a lot.   studying, study, studies

10. Sara does not _____ much.   studying, study, studies

Chapter 2
Distance / Direction

What to do in each section of every lesson...

A - Vocabulary Study

Section A includes the vocabulary that will be used throughout the lesson. Learning new vocabulary is basic to learning a new language.

Read the vocabulary several times.
If you are on Basic ESL Online:
Listen to the **English audio pronunciation**.
View the **native language translations** of the vocabulary.

Listen and read the vocabulary until you can understand the vocabulary without looking at the words.

B - Sentence Structure

Section B teaches students basic English sentences using the vocabulary in section A.

Read and **study** the sentences.
If you are on Basic ESL Online:
Listen to the **English audio pronunciation**.
View the **native language translations** of the sentences.
View the **grammar concepts** by clicking on the **information button** i .

Repeat the sentences as many times as needed. Continue to the next section once you can **understand** the sentences without looking at them.

C - Listening Exercises

Read the story or dialog several times.
If you are on Basic ESL Online, **listen** to the story or dialog while reading it several times.

Once you are familiar with the story or dialog, try to see if you can **understand** it by only listening without reading.

D - Conversation Exercises

Read the conversation dialogs several times.
If you are on Basic ESL Online, **listen** to the dialogs until you can understand them without looking at them.

Finally, try to **speak** the conversation dialogs by only looking at the pictures and key words.

E - Common Phrases

Many of the **common phrases** that are presented in this section are frequently used by the native English speakers in their everyday life.

Read the common phrases several times.
If you are on Basic ESL Online, **listen** to the common phrases while reading. **Listen** as many times as needed until you can understand the common phrases without looking at the sentences.

H - Written Exercises

The written exercises provide an opportunity to test what you learned in the lesson. You can never be sure of knowing something unless you can put it in writing.

You can check your answers by going to the **Answer Key Section** in the back of the workbook.

For information regarding **Basic ESL Online,** please visit **www.basicesl.com**.
Audio Pronunciaton of English & Native Language Translations.

Lesson #4

Distance

Index

Audio & Translations

 English Audio available online for sections A-E.

 Translations in various Languages available online for Sections A, B, and E.

www.BasicESL.com

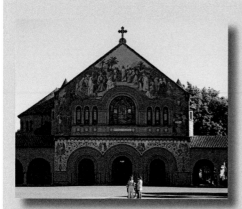

1. church

2. downtown

3. freeway

4. town square

5. avenue

6. river

7. park

8. road

9. bridge

10. palace

11. building

12. castle

13. mountain

14. main street

15. school

16. railroad tracks

17. hill

18. lake

19. next to

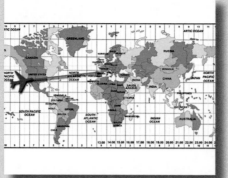

20. far (*from*)

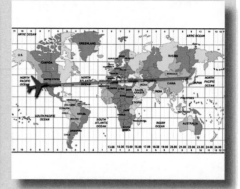

21. very far (*from*)

22. pretty far (*from*)

23. close (*to*)

24. pretty close (*to*)

25.	**30**	thirty
26.	**40**	forty
27.	**50**	fifty
28.	**60**	sixty
29.	**70**	seventy
30.	**80**	eighty
31.	**90**	ninety
32.	**100**	one hundred

Other Vocabulary

1.	n	kilometer	**10.**	v	know
2.	n	meter	**11.**	v	reach
3.	n	mile	**12.**	v	realize
4.	n	university	**13.**	v	think
5.	adj	distant	**14.**	v	travel
6.	adj	exact	**15.**	adv	more
7.	v	achieve	**16.**	adv	now
8.	v	build	**17.**	adv	away
9.	v	climb	**18.**	pre	about

B1. Verb "to be": Past Tense: Affirmative

Singular

I **was** in the park.
He **was** at the restaurant.
She **was** at the store.
It **was** late.
The boy **was** at school.

Plural

We **were** in the church.
You **were** in downtown.
They **were** on the freeway.

B1

*The **past tense** indicates actions that happened in the past. The past tense of the verb **"to be"** is formed with the words "was" and "were".*

B2. Verb "to be": Past Tense: Negative (N)

I **was** in the park.
N   I **was** **not** at the river.

We **were** in the church.
N   We **were** **not** at the school.

You were late.
N   You **were** **not** early.

Lucy **was** at the store.
N   She **was** **not** in the park.

B2 - B3

*Negative sentences with the verb "to be" form the **past tense** by placing the word "not" after the verb form.*

B3. Verb "to be": Present and Past Tense

Today I **am** married.
Yesterday I **was** single.

You **are** happy **now**.
You **were** sad **before**.

He **is** rich **now**.
He **was** poor **before**.

Today we **are** in Mexico.
Yesterday we **were** in Spain.

B4. Questions about Distance: "how far"

How far is downtown?
30   It is **thirty** miles away.

How far is the river?
40   It is **forty** miles away.

How far is the church?
50   It is **fifty** miles away

How far is the freeway?
60   It is **sixty** miles away.

B5. Questions about Distance: "how far"

How far do you live?
70   I live **seventy** miles away.

How far is Mexico?
80   It is **eighty** miles away.

How far do you work?
90   I work **ninety** miles away.

How far is Canada?
100   It is a **hundred** miles away.

B6. Adverbs: Distance

*Is the store **far from** here?*
No, it isn't **very far**.

Is it a mile away?
No, it's not **that far.**

***How close** is it?*
It is **about** half a mile.

*That is not **too** far.*
It is **pretty** close.

B4 - B5

*The questions words "**how far**" or "**how close**" are used to find out the distance between two points.*

C1. Read and Listen to the dialog.

Where do you live?
I live in San Diego, California.

Is San Diego a big city?
Yes it is. It is very big.

How far is it from Los Angeles?
It is around 200 miles away.

Do you live far from Oceanside?
Not too far, about forty miles.

Do you know where Del Mar is?
It is 20 miles away.

Are you studying now?
Yes, I am.

Where are you studying?
At the University of San Diego.

Is it close to your home?
It is close. It is one mile away.

What are you studying?
I'm studying languages.

When do you graduate?
Probably next year.

C2. Read and Listen to the dialog. (Review)

Who likes fruit in your family?
My mom is crazy about fruit.

What fruit does your mom like?
She likes oranges and pears.

What color are the oranges?
They are between red and yellow.

What kind of fruit do you eat?
I eat plums, figs and bananas.

What color are the plums?
They come in different colors:
yellow, red, and purple.

Which ones do you prefer?
I prefer the purple ones.

What fruit do your sisters buy?
They buy apricots, strawberries
and grapes.

D1. you / 1 km / bus

Where were you going?
I was going to church.

How far is the church from here?
It is one kilometer away.

How do you go to church?
I go to church by bus.

D2. Mary / 20 mi / car

Where was Mary going?
She was going to the mountains.

How far are the mountains from here?
They are 20 miles away.

How does she go to the mountains?
She goes to the mountains by car.

D3. children / 100 y / to walk

Where were the children going?
They were going to school.

How far is the school from here?
It is 100 yards away.

How do they go to school?
They go to school walking.

D4. brother / 1/2 mi / to run

Where was your brother going?
He was going to the river.

How far is the river from here?
It is half a mile away.

How does he go to the river?
He goes to the river running.

Useful phrases

1. How does Lucy feel?
2. *She feels so-so.*
3. What do you mean?
4. *It's hard to tell.*
5. *She doesn't complain.*
6. *However, she looks weak.*
7. Perhaps she is sick.
8. *I'm afraid you are wrong.*
9. *I don't see it that way.*
10. *I disagree with you.*

For the English audio pronunciations and written native language translations of **section E,** please go to:

www.basicesl.com

How does Lucy feel?

However, she looks weak.

End of the **oral exercises** for lesson 4.

You can find additional exercises in sections D, F & G at Basic ESL Online.

Please continue with the **written exercises** for this lesson in **section H**.

Lesson
4

H1. Change to the past tense.

1.	I **am** far.	*I was far.*
2.	You are a coward.	
3.	We are going north.	
4.	She is happy.	
5.	They are old.	
6.	Sara is my friend.	
7.	The glasses are full.	

H2. Make the sentence negative. Use the opposite adjective.

1.	They were very **close**.	*They were not far.*
2.	The fence was **high**.	
3.	He was in the **first** row.	
4.	The river was **far**.	
5.	It was an **odd** number.	
6.	She was living **there**.	
7.	My friends were **rich**.	

H3. Write out the numbers.

1.	1	*one*	10	_____
2.	2	_____	20	_____
3.	3	_____	30	_____
4.	4	_____	40	_____
5.	5	_____	50	_____
6.	6	_____	60	_____
7.	7	_____	70	_____
8.	8	_____	80	_____
9.	9	_____	90	_____
10.	0	_____	100	_____

H4. Make contractions.

1. They **were not** close.   *They **weren't** close.*

2. The fence was not high. _____

3. He was not in the first row. _____

4. The men were not far. _____

5. It was not an odd number. _____

6. She was not living there. _____

7. My friends were not rich. _____

8. The hat was not expensive. _____

H5. Choose the correct answer.

1.	Circle the even numbers.	52	13	16	18
2.	Underline the odd numbers.	7	10	11	25
3.	Write the missing number.	45	50	_____	60
4.	A very short distance.	---	------	=	----------
5.	_____ is in the east.	Denver	New York	Chicago	Dallas
6.	Chicago is a _____ city.	southern	western	eastern	northern

H6. Make Questions.

1. Tony was working. *Was Tony working?*
2. We were watching TV. _____
3. He knows the distance. _____
4. The palace was far away. _____
5. She has three rulers. _____
6. There was a lot of traffic. _____
7. They underline the words. _____
8. They were two miles away. _____
9. It was not far. _____
10. You realize that. _____
11. He climbs that hill. _____

H7. Follow the example.

1. you / downtown / 70 mi

   river

   Where were you yesterday?
   I was in downtown.
   How far is downtown from the river?
   It is seventy miles away.

2. Jane / mountain / 40 mi

   freeway

   _____

   _____

   _____

3. the children / school / 90 yd

   park

   _____

   _____

   _____

4. John / palace / 50 km

   lake

   _____

   _____

   _____

Lesson #5

Direction

Index

Audio & Translations

 English Audio available online for sections A-E.

 Translations in various Languages available online for Sections A, B, and E.

www.BasicESL.com

1. north

2. south

3. east

4. west

5. eastern (*city*)

6. western (*city*)

7. northern (*city*)

8. southern (*city*)

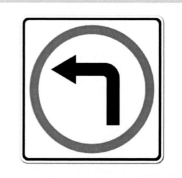

9. left

10. right

11. straight ahead

12. one way only

13. that way

14. this way

15. towards (*the mountain*)

16. through (*the mountain*)

17. forward

18. backwards

19. upward

20. downward

Other Vocabulary

1.	n	capital	**10.**	v	make
2.	n	path	**11.**	v	plan
3.	n	route	**12.**	v	visit
4.	n	state	**13.**	v	cut across
5.	n	trip	**14.**	v	agree
6.	n	way	**15.**	v	arrive
7.	adj	opposite	**16.**	v	begin
8.	adj	wrong	**17.**	adv	yesterday
9.	v	continue	**18.**	pre	across

For the audio pronunciations and written translations of **Sections A and B,** please go to:

www.basicesl.com

B1. Verb "to be": Past Tense: Questions (Q)

i

You **were** at the store.
Q   **Were** you at the store?

He **was** in downtown.
Q   **Was** he in downtown?

She **was** at the restaurant.
Q   **Was** she at the restaurant?

They **were** on the roof.
Q   **Were** they on the roof?

B2. Verb "to be": Past Tense: Progressive Form

What **were** you **doing**?
I **was climbing** the mountain.

Where **was** Greg **studying**?
He **was studying** at home.

Where **were** they **driving**?
They **were driving** to Chicago.

Who **was driving** the car?
My mom **was driving** the car.

B3. Past Tense: Negative Sentences: Contractions (C)

i

Were you visiting Dallas?
No, I **was not** visiting Dallas.
C   No, I **wasn't** visiting Dallas.

Was Charles sleeping?
No, he **was not** sleeping.
C   No, he **wasn't** sleeping.

Were the children playing?
No, they **were not** playing.
C   No, they **weren't** playing.

B1 - B2

*With the verb "to be", **questions** in the **past tense** are formed by placing the verb **in front of** the subject.*

B3 - B4

*With the verb "to be", **negative sentences** in English are formed by placing the word "not" after the verb "**to be**".*

*A **contraction** is the union of two words into one, separated by an apostrophe ('). With the verb "to be", "**was not**" and "**were not**" can be contracted into "**wasn't**" and "**weren't**".*

B4. Past Tense: Negative sentences: Contractions (C)

Were you at the store?
No, I **was not** at the store.
C   No, I **wasn't** at the store.

Was I sleeping?
No, you **were not** sleeping.
C   No, you **weren't** sleeping.

Were they at the university?
No, they **were not** there.
C   No, they **weren't** there.

B3 - B4 (continued)

B5. Direction: Question Words: "which way"

Which way is the river?
The river is in the opposite direction.

Which is the way to the castle?
It is this way.

Which way were the girls going?
They were going south.

Is this the way to the palace?
No, this is the wrong way.

B5

When we want to inquire about the direction that someone or something is going, we use the question words "which way".

B6. Location: Question Words: "where"

Where is Florida?
It is in the southeast.

Where is New York?
It is in the northeast.

Where is Arizona?
It is in the southwest.

Where is Washington State?
It is in the northwest.

B6

When we want to inquire about the location of someone or something we use the question word "where".

C1. Read and Listen to the story of Janet and I.

Janet and I are making plans to visit southern California. **Our** parents like to visit northern California. **Janet and** I begin our trip in Los Angeles. **We** plan to drive from Los Angeles to San Francisco. There are two freeways going to San Francisco. Freeway 5 cuts across the state from north to south.

Janet and I prefer this route because **we** have a friend in Fresno. From Fresno **we** continue **our** trip to San Francisco. **We** pass through Sacramento. **We** plan to visit the capital of the state on **our** way back from San Francisco.

C2. Read and Listen to the story.

My family lives in a big house. The house is not too old. It's only ten years old. It is a beautiful house. It has a patio and a porch in front of the house. My family enjoys the backyard of the house. My sister and I play in the backyard. My mom likes to sit on the porch and read books. My dad likes to work in the backyard.

Our house has five bedrooms and three bathrooms. One bathroom and one of the bedrooms are downstairs. The other four bedrooms and two bathrooms are upstairs. My parents have a master bedroom with its own bathroom inside.

D1. Paul / Denver/ Bismark

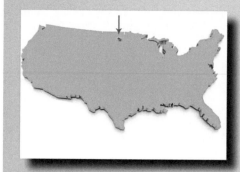

Tomorrow Paul is leaving Denver.
He is going to Bismark.

Where is Bismark?
It is in the north. It is a northern city.

Which way is he going?
He doesn't know yet.

D2. I / N.Y. / L.A.

Tomorrow I am leaving New York.
I am going to Los Angeles.

Where is Los Angeles?
It is in the west. It is a western city.

Which way are you going?
I don't know yet.

D3. Mary / Dallas / Houston

Tomorrow Mary is leaving Dallas.
She is going to Houston.

Where is Houston?
It is in the south. It is a southern city.

Which way is she going?
She doesn't know yet.

D4. we / Georgia / Richmond

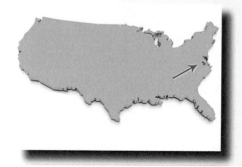

Tomorrow we are leaving Georgia.
We are going to Richmond.

Where is Richmond?
It is in the east. It is an eastern city.

Which way are we going?
We don't know yet.

Feeling Pain

1. Is anything wrong with you?
2. *My arm hurts.*
3. How much does it hurt?
4. *It hurts a lot.*
5. Do you take any medicine?
6. *No, I don't.*
7. Why don't you go to the doctor?
8. *I plan to go early tomorrow.*
9. Don't wait any longer.
10. The sooner the better.

For the English audio pronunciations and written native language translations of **section E,** please go to:

www.basicesl.com

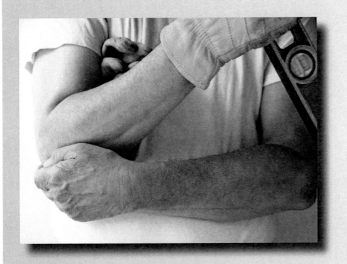

My arm hurts

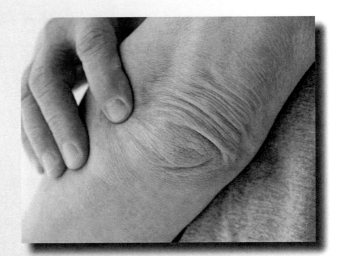

It hurts a lot.

End of the **oral exercises** for lesson 5.
You can find additional exercises in sections D, F & G at Basic ESL Online.

Please continue with the **written exercises** for this lesson in **section H.**

Lesson

5

H1. Write the opposite.

1. east	*west*	
2. south	_____	
3. northern	_____	
4. western	_____	
5. many	_____	
6. much	_____	

7. right	_____	
8. near	_____	
9. close	_____	
10. first	_____	
11. more	_____	
12. next	_____	

H2. Change to the past tense.

1. I **am** going to the store.   *I **was** going to the store.*

2. I'm not going home.   _____

3. You're studying hard.   _____

4. You're not playing a lot.   _____

5. Greg is going west.   _____

6. He's not going east.   _____

H3. Make the sentences plural.

1. The child is sleeping.

    The children are sleeping.

2. The man was far away.

    _____

3. A woman prepares the meal.

    _____

4. She prefers a gray skirt.

    _____

5. I wasn't at home.

    _____

6. This is your last grade.

    _____

7. That's a big potato.

    _____

8. The girl is nice.

    _____

9. He likes the sausages.

    _____

10. The child is sleeping.

    _____

11. He cleans the dirty dish.

    _____

H4. Complete with quantity adjectives: *many, a lot, lots of, much, little, few.*

1. How *many* bars of soap do you have? I have _____ .

2. Do you use _____ salt? Some foods have _____ of salt.

3. Do you see _____ pieces of chalk? I see quite a _____ .

4. I have _____ of apples, but I don't have _____ oranges.

5. There is _____ room on the shelves for_____ books.

6. It contains _____ books. There is _____ of room for more.

7. Sara cries _____ at night. Lucy doesn't cry _____ .

8. My brothers eat _____ of pie. _____ pies are not good.

9. There is not _____ milk there. There is _____ of milk here.

10. How _____ time do you have? I have a _____ hours .

H5. Follow the example.

1. you / 50 miles

    Boston east

    Where is Boston?
        It's in the east.

    Is Boston an eastern city?
        Yes, it is.

    How far from Boston do you live?
        I live fifty miles away from Boston.

2. Liz / 60 miles

    San Francisco west

    _____
    _____
    _____
    _____
    _____
    _____

3. parents / 40 miles

    Houston south

    _____
    _____
    _____
    _____
    _____
    _____

4. sister / 80 miles

    Chicago north

    _____
    _____
    _____
    _____
    _____
    _____

H6. Write the same story changing *Janet and I* for *Janet*.

Janet and I are making plans to visit northern California. **We** begin **our** trip in Los Angeles. **We** are taking freeway 5 to San Francisco.

Janet and I prefer this route because **we** have a friend in Fresno. From there **we** continue **our** trip to San Francisco.

We pass through Sacramento, the capital of the state. **We** plan to visit this city on **our** way back to Los Angeles.

Janet _____

_____

_____

_____

_____

_____

_____

_____

_____

_____

_____

_____

_____

H7. Answer the questions about the story above.

1. What does Janet want to see?

   _____

2. Where does the trip start?

   _____

3. Where is she planning to go?

   _____

4. Why does she prefer to take the freeway 5?

   _____

5. Is she planning to visit Sacramento before going to San Francisco?

   _____

Lesson #6

Giving Directions

Index

Audio & Translations

 English Audio available online for sections A-E.

 Translations in various Languages available online for Sections A, B, and E.

www.BasicESL.com

1. cross (*the street*)

2. turn (*right*)

3. wait for (*the bus*)

4. get on (*the bus*)

5. pay (*for the ticket*)

6. take (*a seat*)

7. pass (*a traffic light*)

8. ring (*the bell*)

9. stand up

10. get off (*the bus*)

11. turn (*left*)

12. walk (*one block*)

13. go (*straight ahead*)

14. wait for (*the light*)

15.	11	eleven
16.	22	twenty-two
17.	33	thirty-three
18.	44	forty-four
19.	55	fifty-five
20.	66	sixty-six
21.	77	seventy-seven
22.	88	eighty-eight
23.	99	ninety-nine

Other Vocabulary

1.	n	corner	10.	v	calculate
2.	n	hospital	11.	v	command
3.	n	instruction	12.	v	give
4.	n	light	13.	v	own
5.	n	row	14.	v	stand
6.	n	side	15.	v	stop
7.	n	suggestion	16.	v	turn
8.	n	town	17.	v	change
9.	adj	various	18.	pre	to

For the audio pronunciations and written translations of **Sections A and B**, please go to:

www.basicesl.com

Looking for Bilingual Dictionaries?
You can find a large selection at:

www.bilingualdictionaries.com

B1. Imperative Sentences: Commands

Get on bus #5.
Don't get on bus #10.

Pass three traffic lights.
Don't pass four traffic lights.

Get off at downtown.
Don't get off at the hospital.

Cross Broadway Avenue.
Don't cross Main Street.

B2. Imperative Sentences: Requests

Please, go straight ahead.
Don't turn left.

Please, take the next bus.
Don't sit in the back.

Please, sit down on an empty seat.
Don't stand up by the door.

Please, walk ahead five blocks.
The market is on your left side.

B3. Suggestions: Affirmative and Negative

Let us go home.
Let us not go to the river.

Let us visit our mom.
Let us not visit our nephews.

Let us work hard.
Let us not be lazy.

Let us mend our clothes.
Let us not buy new clothes.

B1 - B2

*Imperative sentences express **direct commands**, **requests** or **suggestions**. The subject is always **"you"** in direct commands and requests, although the subject is not present in the sentence.*

B3 - B4

*Suggestions are expressed with the words **"let us."** The subject of the sentence is always **"we"**, although it is not present in the subject form.*

B4. Suggestions: Contractions

Let us prepare for the test.
Let's prepare for the test.

Let us cross out the mistakes.
Let's cross out the mistakes.

Let us use pencils only.
Let's use pencils only.

Let us be quiet during the test.
Let's be quiet during the test.

B3 - B4 (continued)

The contraction of "let us" is "let's."

B5. Indefinite Adjectives: "several, other, another"

I have **several** cups.
One is dirty.
Other cups are old.
The others are clean.
I need **another** one at least.

I want **several** plates.
I only have two plates.
One is ugly.
The other is broken.
Please, buy **another** plate.

B6. Quantity Adjectives: "less, fewer"

How many people are there?
There are **fewer** people.
They have **less** interest now.

How many dollars do you have?
I have **fewer** dollars.
I spend **less** money now.

How many times do you go there?
I go there **fewer** times.
I have **less** time to go there.

B6 (Review)

C1. Read and Listen to the Story.

My cousin is new in town. **He** likes to know various places: the church, the library, the river, the downtown area and the main square. **He** wants to go by bus. These were my **instructions:**

When **you** leave the house, **cross** the street and turn right. **Walk** to the bus stop and then **wait** for the bus. When the bus arrives, **get on** the bus and pay for the ticket. **Give** the exact change. **Take a seat** and pass two traffic lights. Then, **stand up** and ring the bell. When the door opens, **get off** the bus and turn left.

C2. Read and Listen to the Story.

Janet and I are new in town. **We** like to know various places: the church, the library, the river, the downtown area and the main square. **We want** to go by bus. These were my **suggestions:**

When **we** leave the house, **let us cross** the street and turn right. **Let us walk** to the bus stop and **let us wait** for the bus. When the bus arrives, **let us get** on the bus and pay for the ticket. Then, **let us give** the exact change. **Let us take** a seat and pass two traffic lights. **Let us stand** up and ring the bell. When the door opens, **let us get off** the bus and turn left.

D1. Give directions

park / Town Hall

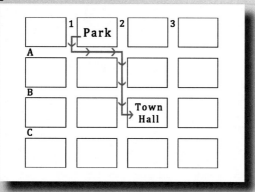

I am at the park.
How do I get to the Town Hall?

Walk to the corner of A Ave.

Turn left and walk one block.

Cross 2nd Street.

Turn right and cross A Avenue.

Keep on walking one block.

Turn left on B Avenue.

Walk another block.

Turn right and cross B Avenue.

The Town Hall is on your left.

D2. Give directions

home / church

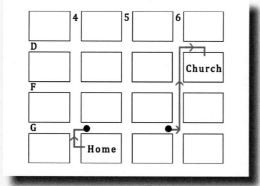

I am at home.
How do I get to the church?

When you leave home turn right.

Walk to the corner of G Street.

Take the bus at the bus stop.

Get off the bus at the next stop.

Turn left and cross 6th Street.

Turn left and cross G Avenue.

Walk straight two blocks.

Turn right at D Street.

The church is not far away.

Instructions

1. **How do I get to school?**
2. *Go to the bus stop.*
3. *Take bus number 20.*
4. *Pass two traffic lights.*
5. *Get off the bus at Park Avenue.*
6. *Turn right and cross the street.*
7. *Turn left.*
8. *Walk one block.*
9. *Cross "D" street.*
10. *The school is on your left side.*

For the English audio pronunciations and written native language translations of **section E,** please go to:

www.basicesl.com

Go to bus stop.

Walk one block.

End of the **oral exercises** for lesson 6.
You can find additional exercises in sections D, F & G at Basic ESL Online.

Please continue with the **written exercises** for this lesson in **section H.**

Lesson 6

H1. Make negative commands or suggestions.

1. Open the book.
2. Let us close books.
3. Let us start the test
4. Get on the bus.
5. Let us take a seat.
6. Take a seat.
7. Let us stand up.
8. Ring the bell.

Do not open the book.

_____

_____

_____

_____

_____

_____

_____

H2. Make contractions.

1. Do not turn left.
2. Let us not sit down.
3. Do not get on the bus.
4. Let us not walk.
5. Do not take a seat.
6. Let us not wait for the bus.
7. Do not take bus no. 40.

Don't turn left.

_____

_____

_____

_____

_____

_____

H3. Make commands.

1. wait / bus / train

   Wait for the bus. Don't wait for the train.

2. go / school / home

   _____

3. take / shirt / T-shirt

   _____

4. get / bus 40 / bus 50

   _____

5. write / pen / pencil

   _____

6. turn / left / right

   _____

H4. Write the math operations.

1.   55   _____
2.   -22   _____
3.   =33   _____

4.   44   _____
5.   x2   _____
6.   =88   _____

7.   66   _____
8.   +11   _____
9.   =77   _____

H5. Ask the questions corresponding to these answers.

Answer	Corresponding Question
1. Your uncle was **fat**.	*What* was your uncle *like?*
2. Ann eats **a lot of** meat.	
3. **Her aunt** is thin.	
4. The church was **very close**.	
5. **The church** is beautiful.	
6. Ann goes to church **this way**.	
7. Mary is in **the kitchen**.	
8. She's eating **pancakes**.	
9. Her sister likes **fish**.	
10. Tony eats **few** sandwiches.	
11. His shirt is **blue**.	
12. **The sweater** is brown.	
13. Sara was **two miles** away.	
14. Tony was **two** miles away.	
15. Henry has **lots of** lamps.	
16. Mary uses **a lot of** sugar.	
17. **Fred** is wrong.	
18. He is **eleven years** old.	
19. Mary is traveling to **France**.	
20. It is **very far**.	
21. Two and two are **four**.	
22. Mary is **smart and tall**.	
23. She was going **south**.	
24. She was driving **10 mph**.	

H6. Give directions about how to go from the bus station to the hospital.

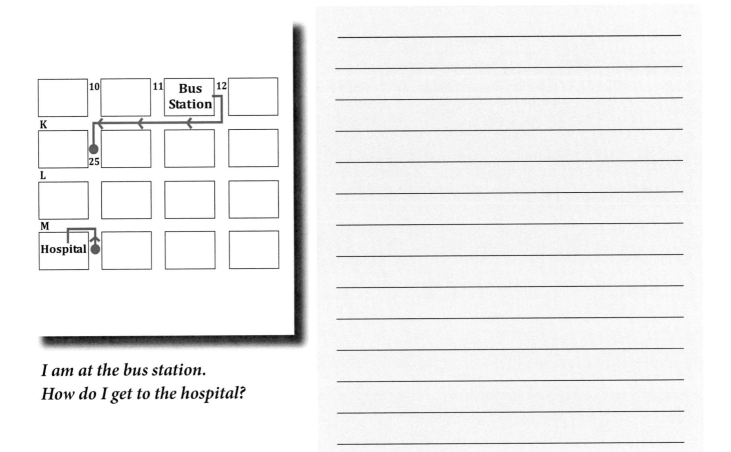

I am at the bus station.
How do I get to the hospital?

_____

_____

_____

_____

_____

_____

_____

_____

_____

_____

_____

_____

H7. Multiple choice. Select the correct answer.

1. Paula _____ not at home today.   **is**, was, are, were
2. Joe _____ not at home yesterday.   is, was, are, were
3. We _____ not at home the day before.   is, was, are, were
4. They _____ not at home every day.   is, was, are, were
5. How _____ is the market from here?   many, far, old, way
6. Which _____ do you go there?   many, far, old, way
7. How _____ miles away are you?   many, far, old, way
8. _____ wants to go with Richard?   From, Who, Through
9. He enters the house _____ the window.   from, who, through
10. My family comes _____ Mexico.   from, who, always

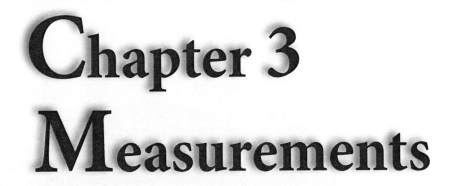

Chapter 3
Measurements

Lesson 7:   Length, Width, Depth
Lesson 8:   Weight
Lesson 9:   Money

What to do in each section of every lesson...

A - Vocabulary Study

Section A includes the vocabulary that will be used throughout the lesson. Learning new vocabulary is basic to learning a new language.

Read the vocabulary several times.
If you are on Basic ESL Online:
Listen to the **English audio pronunciation**.
View the **native language translations** of the vocabulary.

Listen and read the vocabulary until you can understand the vocabulary without looking at the words.

B - Sentence Structure

Section B teaches students basic English sentences using the vocabulary in section A.

Read and **study** the sentences.
If you are on Basic ESL Online:
Listen to the **English audio pronunciation**.
View the **native language translations** of the sentences.
View the **grammar concepts** by clicking on the **information button** .

Repeat the sentences as many times as needed. Continue to the next section once you can **understand** the sentences without looking at them.

C - Listening Exercises

Read the story or dialog several times.
If you are on Basic ESL Online, **listen** to the story or dialog while reading it several times.

Once you are familiar with the story or dialog, try to see if you can **understand** it by only listening without reading.

D - Conversation Exercises

Read the conversation dialogs several times.
If you are on Basic ESL Online, **listen** to the dialogs until you can understand them without looking at them.

Finally, try to **speak** the conversation dialogs by only looking at the pictures and key words.

E - Common Phrases

Many of the **common phrases** that are presented in this section are frequently used by the native English speakers in their everyday life.

Read the common phrases several times.
If you are on Basic ESL Online, **listen** to the common phrases while reading. **Listen** as many times as needed until you can understand the common phrases without looking at the sentences.

H - Written Exercises

The written exercises provide an opportunity to test what you learned in the lesson. You can never be sure of knowing something unless you can put it in writing.

You can check your answers by going to the **Answer Key Section** in the back of the workbook.

For information regarding **Basic ESL Online**, please visit **www.basicesl.com**.
Audio Pronunciaton of English & Native Language Translations.

Lesson #7

Length, Width & Depth

Index

Audio & Translations

English Audio available online for sections A-E.

Translations in various Languages available online for Sections A, B, and E.

www.BasicESL.com

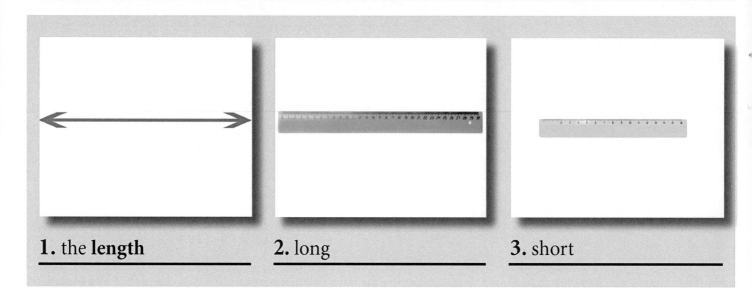

1. the **length**

2. long

3. short

4. the **depth**

5. deep

6. shallow

7. the **width**

8. wide

9. narrow

10. the **height**

11. tall

12. short

13. the **height** (*altitude*)

14. high

15. low

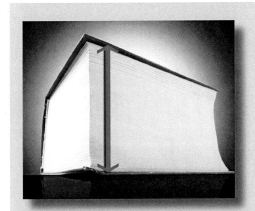

16. the **thickness**

17. thick

18. thin

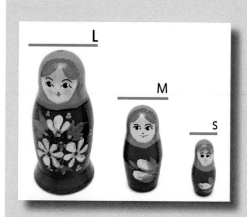

19. the **size**

20. large

21. small

Other Vocabulary

1.	n	foot	10.	v	lift
2.	n	inch	11.	v	list
3.	adj	yard	12.	v	measure
4.	adj	medium	13.	v	promise
5.	adj	regular	14.	v	recognize
6.	adj	tiny	15.	v	pull
7.	v	collect	16.	v	push
8.	v	compare	17.	adv	at least
9.	v	fill	18.	adv	enough

For the audio pronunciations and written translations of **Sections A and B,** please go to:

www.basicesl.com

Looking for Bilingual Dictionaries?
You can find a large selection at:

www.bilingualdictionaries.com

B1. Regular Verbs (RV): Past Tense

fill	I fill**ed** the box.
lift	You lift**ed** the flag.
push	He push**ed** the car.
open	She open**ed** the door.
work	It work**ed** fine.
peel	They peel**ed** the oranges.
complain	We complain**ed** a lot.
gain	Anne gain**ed** weight.

B1

Regular verbs are those that form the past tense and the past participle by adding "-ed" to the basic form of verb.

B2. RV: Past Tense: Verbs ending in "-e"

serve	I serv**ed** the tables.
place	You plac**ed** the keys here.
taste	He tast**ed** the soup.
survive	She surviv**ed** the crash.
arrive	The train arriv**ed** late.
realize	We realiz**ed** this late.
continue	Harry continu**ed** walking.
promise	They promis**ed** that.

B2

Verbs ending in "-e" (silent) lose the "-e" before adding "-ed."

B3. RV: Past Tense: Verbs ending in "-y"

carry	Mom carr**ied** the baby.
copy	Sue cop**ied** the test.
cry	She cr**ied** a lot.
fry	He fr**ied** the steaks.
worry	We worr**ied** a lot.
study	I stud**ied** for the test.
delay	They delay**ed** the trip.
stay	John stay**ed** at home.

B3

Verbs ending in "-y" preceded by a consonant, change the "-y" into "-i" before adding "-ed."

B4. RV: Past Tense: Double Consonant

Verb	Past Tense
stir	Mom stir**red** the soup.
trim	You trim**med** the fat.
chop	He chop**ped** the onions.
wrap	She wrap**ped** the meat.
stop	It stop**ped** working.
plan	I plan**ned** to see you.

B4

*For one syllable verbs ending in a **consonant** preceded by a single vowel, you must **double** the consonant before adding "-ed."*

B5. Question Words: Measurements

What was the width of the door?
How wide was the door?

What was your height before?
How tall were you?

What is the thickness of the book?
How thick is the book?

What is the depth of the river?
How deep is the river?

B5 - B6

*When we want to obtain information about measurements (length, width, height, etc.) we can use two different types of **question words**:*

1. *"What + noun..."*

2. *"How + adjective..."*

B6. Question Words: Measurements

What is the wealth of Peter?
How wealthy is Peter?

What size is the table?
How large (big) is the table?

What is the thinness of the pen?
How thin is the pen?

What is the height of the mountain?
How high is the mountain?

C1. Read and Listen to the story.

My teacher has a big desk in the classroom. I don't know its exact measurements. Its length is about five feet. Its width is about three feet and its height is about two and a half feet.

There are three things on the desk: a dictionary, a textbook and a notebook. The dictionary is very thick. It is eleven inches long, eight inches wide and three inches thick. Both the notebook and the textbook are regular size. They are eight and a half inches wide by eleven inches long.

There is also a wastebasket near the desk. It is not very deep. I don't know its exact depth.

C2. Read and Listen to the dialog.

What is the table of the teacher like?
It is big.

How long is the desk?
It is five feet long.

How wide is it?
It is three feet wide.

How high is the desk?
It is two and a half feet high.

What do you see on the table?
I see a book and a notebook.

How thick is the book?
It is three inches thick.

Is the notebook thick too?
No, it is thin.

What size is the notebook?
I don't know its exact size.

Is it a regular size?
I think so.

Thank you for the information.
Don't mention it.

D1. 25" width / you / 32"

How wide is the TV?
It is 25" wide, more or less.

Is it wide enough for you?
No, it isn't. It is a little narrow.

What width do you prefer?
I prefer a width of 32 inches.

D2. 20' length / Diane / 32'

How long is the bus?
It is 20 feet long, more or less.

Is it long enough for Diane?
No, it isn't. It is a little short.

What length does Diane prefer?
She prefers a length of 32 feet.

D3. 1" thickness / Mary / 2"

How thick is the book?
It is 1" thick, more or less.

Is it thick enough for Mary?
No, it isn't. It is a little thin.

What thickness does Mary prefer?
She prefers a thickness of 2 inches.

D4. 1' depth / boys / 4'

How deep is the river?
It is 1' deep, more or less.

Is it deep enough for the boys?
No it isn't. It is a little shallow.

What depth do the boys prefer?
They prefer a depth of 4 feet.

Shopping

1. How much is this shirt?
2. *The regular price is $20.*
3. *Today it is on sale.*
4. What is the discount?
5. *It is 25% off the regular price.*
6. I'll take it.
7. *Anything else?*
8. No, that's all.
9. *How do you want to pay?*
10. I want to pay cash.

For the English audio pronunciations and written native language translations of **section E,** please go to:

www.basicesl.com

I want to pay cash.

It is on sale.

End of the **oral exercises** for lesson 7.
You can find additional exercises in sections D, F & G at Basic ESL Online.

Please continue with the **written exercises** for this lesson in **section H**.

Lesson

7

H1. Form the past tense of these regular verbs.

1.	bless	*blessed*	achieve	_____
2.	carry	_____	calculate	_____
3.	close	_____	chop	_____
4.	collect	_____	copy	_____
5.	compare	_____	fade	_____
6.	delay	_____	gain	_____
7.	fill	_____	lift	_____
8.	fry	_____	plan	_____
9.	mix	_____	promise	_____
10.	open	_____	cry	_____
11.	pull	_____	stay	_____
12.	study	_____	stir	_____
13.	trim	_____	stop	_____
14.	walk	_____	wait	_____
15.	worry	_____	wash	_____
16.	cross	_____	change	_____

H2. Change to the past tense.

Every day	Yesterday	
1. He **opens** the door.	*He **opened*** _____	the door.
2. We wait for the bus.	_____	for the bus.
3. The bus stops here.	_____	here.
4. Mary washes the fruit.	_____	the fruit.
5. I visit my uncles.	_____	my uncles.
6. Mom trims the fat.	_____	the fat.
7. Sara studies at school.	_____	at school.
8. The child cries at night.	_____	at night.
9. They ask questions.	_____	questions.
10. They copy the tests.	_____	the tests.
11. He fills the glass.	_____	the glass.
12. Susan fries the chicken.	_____	the chicken.
13. They stay at home.	_____	at home.
14. They cry at home.	_____	cry at home.
15. Mom chops the onions.	_____	the onions.
16. I worry about you.	_____	about you.
17. Carol washes the clothes.	_____	the clothes.
18. This fabric is cheap.	_____	cheap.
19. We study at night.	_____	at night.
20. The man blesses the food.	_____	the food.
21. I plan to see you.	_____	you.
22. Dad trims the fat.	_____	the fat.
23. My aunt stirs the soup.	_____	the soup.
24. She mixes the fruit.	_____	the fruit.

H3. Ask the corresponding questions.

Answer	Corresponding Question
1. The table is **3'** long.	*How **long** is the table?* *What's **the length** of the table?*
2. The desk is **1'** wide.	
3. Henry is **5'4"** tall.	
4. The river is **2'** deep.	
5. The building is **30'** high.	
6. Diane is **17 years** old.	
7. The ruler is **12"** long.	
8. The table is **big**.	

H4. Rewrite the story. Change *every day* for *last year*.

Every day Mrs. Gray **prepares** the dinners. She usually **cooks** meat or turkey for dinner. There **is** plenty of meat or chicken in the freezer, but there **are** not many vegetables.

The big family **starts** dinner with a bowl of soup. The children **like** homemade soup mainly, especially chicken soup. They **hate** canned soup.

After eating the soup, Mrs. Gray **serves** the main course. It **consists** of meat with potatoes, rice or green vegetables.

There **are** always some desserts for dinner. Their favorite one **is** ice-cream.

Last year _____

_____

_____

_____

_____

_____

_____

_____

_____

_____

_____

_____

_____

_____

_____

_____

_____

_____

_____

Lesson #8

Weight

Index

Audio & Translations

English Audio available online for sections A-E.

Translations in various Languages available online for Sections A, B, and E.

www.BasicESL.com

1. the volume

2. quart (*of oil*)

3. gallon (*of milk*)

4. liter (*of wine*)

5. pint (*of milk*)

6. the weight

7. pound

8. half-pound

9. ounce

10. kilogram (*kilo*)

11. gram

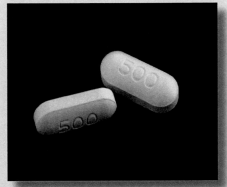

12. milligram

13. 5 gallon bottle

14. 2 liter bottle

15. 12 ounce can

16. light (*feather*)

17. heavy (*box*)

18. very heavy (box)

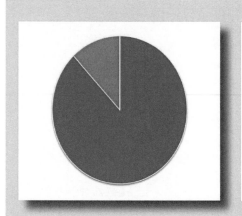

13. part

14. whole

15.	200	two hundred
16.	300	three hundred
17.	400	four hundred
18.	500	five hundred
19.	600	six hundred
20.	700	seven hundred
21.	800	eight hundred
22.	900	nine hundred
23.	1000	one thousand

Other Vocabulary

1.	n	corner	10.	v	calculate
2.	n	hospital	11.	v	command
3.	n	instruction	12.	v	give
4.	n	light	13.	v	own
5.	n	row	14.	v	stand
6.	n	side	15.	v	stop
7.	n	suggestion	16.	v	turn
8.	n	town	17.	v	change
9.	adj	various	18.	pre	to

For the audio pronunciations and written translations of **Sections A and B,** please go to:

www.basicesl.com

Looking for Bilingual Dictionaries?
You can find a large selection at:

www.bilingualdictionaries.com

B1. RV: Past Tense: **Negative Contractions (NC)**

Aff	I weigh**ed** 90 pounds.
Neg	I **did not weigh** 80 pounds.
NC	I **didn't weigh** 80 pounds.

Aff	Mike carri**ed** a heavy suitcase.
Neg	He **did not carry** a light suitcase.
NC	He **didn't carry** a light suitcase.

Aff	Alice lift**ed** the chair.
Neg	She **did not lift** the table.
NC	She **didn't lift** the table.

B1 - B2

RV - Regular Verbs

Negative Statements in the past tense are formed with *"did not"* in front of the verb. The form of the verb is the same for all subjects. In the negative form, *"-ed"* is not added to the verb. The contraction of *"did not"* is *"didn't."*

B2. RV: Past Tense: **Negative Contractions**

Sara gain**ed** some weight.
She **did not gain** much weight.
She **didn't gain** too much weight.
She only gain**ed** a little weight.

I ask**ed** so many questions.
I **did not ask** many questions.
I **didn't ask** too many questions.
I only **asked** a few questions.

B3. Questions About Weight

Is the box too **heavy**?
No, it is very light.

How much does it weigh?
It weighs 60 pounds. (60 lbs)

How much do you weigh?
I weigh 130 pounds.

What is your weight?
My weight is 130 pounds.

B4. RV: Past Tense: Pronunciation of "-ed"

Past Tense	T	ED	D	Past Tense	T	ED	D
I ask**ed**.	X			I wash**ed**.	X		
I call**ed**.			X	I chopp**ed**.			X
I dress**ed**.	X			I add**ed**.		X	
I lift**ed**.		X		I mix**ed**.	X		
I lik**ed**.	X			I blend**ed**.		X	
I work**ed**.	X			I peel**ed**.			X
I cross**ed**.	X			I remov**ed**.			X
I pull**ed**.			X	I push**ed**.	X		

B4

"-ed" is pronounced like "t" when the verb ends in sounds of "s, sh, x, ch or k."

"-ed" is pronounced like "ed" when the verb ends in sounds of "t" or "d."

"-ed" is pronounced like "d" in all other cases.

B5. Noun Substitution: "one" or "ones"

I want a white **car**.
I don't want an orange **one**.

She sleeps in the soft **bed**.
She doesn't sleep in the hard **one**.

She prefers pink **robes**.
She doesn't prefer green **ones**.

The gray **shoes** are cheap.
The black **ones** are expensive.

B5 (Review)

B6. Phrase "there is, there are": Negative Statements

Aff.	**There are** many pies there.
Neg	**There aren't any** pies there.
Neg	**There are no** pies there.
Aff	Today **there is** soup.
Neg	Today **there isn't any** soup.
Neg	Today **there is no** soup.
Aff	**There is** tea for breakfast.
Neg	**There isn't any** tea for lunch.
Neg	**There is no** tea for lunch.

B6 (Review)

C1. Listening Exercise: Listen to the story in the **past tense.**

Last year Henry wa**lked** to the lake. His friends **accompanied** him to the lake.

Last year Henry **preferred** to buy five pounds of meat. His friends **wanted** to bring some fish. All **agreed** on the salad and the drinks.

Last year when they **arrived** at the lake, they **rested** on the grass. Later, they **crossed** the lake in a boat and **started** fishing. There **was** plenty of fish for everybody. Some of the fish **weighed** five pounds. Others **weighed** half a pound or a few ounces. Henry **cooked** the fish. It **tasted** very good.

C2. Listening Exercise: Listen to the same story in the **present tense.**

Every year Henry **walks** to the lake. His friends **accompany** him to the lake.

Every year Henry **prefers** to buy 5 pounds of meat. His friends **want** to bring some fish. All **agree** on the salad and the drinks.

Every year when they **arrive** at the lake, they **rest** on the grass. Later, they **cross** the lake in a boat and **start** fishing. There **is** plenty of fish for everybody. Some of the fish **weighs** five pounds. Others **weigh** half a pound or a few ounces. Henry **cooks** the fish. It **tastes** very good.

D1. Mike / need / milk 22 gal.

Mike needs many gallons of milk.
Yesterday he needed 22 gallons.

Today he is not needing that many.
He only needs a few.

Does he drink a lot of milk?
  Sometimes he does.

D2. they / ask / beer 33 pt.

They ask for many pints of beer.
Yesterday they asked for 33 pints.

Today they are not asking for that many.
They only need a few.

Do they drink a lot of beer?
  Sometimes they do.

D3. mom / purchase / figs 44 lb.

Mom purchases many pounds of figs.
Yesterday she purchased 44 pounds.

Today she is not purchasing that many.
She only needs a few.

Does she eat lots of figs?
  Sometimes she does.

D4. I / order / nuts 7 kg.

I order many kilos of nuts.
Yesterday I ordered 7 kilos.

Today I am not ordering that many.
I only need a few.

Do you eat lots of nuts?
  Sometimes I do.

Giving Advice

1. I need some help.
2. *What can I do for you?*
3. I'm planning to quit school.
4. I don't feel like studying.
5. *Are your parents upset?*
6. Yes, they are. I need your advice.
7. *First of all, you are wrong.*
8. *Your parents are right.*
9. *You should stay in school.*
10. *Make up your mind. Don't put it off.*

For the English audio pronunciations and written native language translations of **section E,** please go to:

www.basicesl.com

I need some help.

Make up your mind. Don't put it off.

End of the **oral exercises** for lesson 8.
You can find additional exercises in sections D, F & G at Basic ESL Online.

Please continue with the **written exercises** for this lesson in **section H**.

H - Written Exercises

8-10

Lesson 8

H1. Make the sentences *negative*.

Affirmative	Negative	
1. She **peeled** the tomatoes.	*She **did not peel***	the tomatoes.
2. I removed the seeds.		the seeds.
3. You lifted the flag.		the flag.
4. Tom trimmed the fat.		the fat.
5. We loved the school.		the school.
6. They called the teacher.		the teacher.
7. I chopped the onions.		the onions.
8. He walked to the river.		to the river.
9. He stopped at the store.		at the store.
10. They washed the fruit.		the fruit.
11. They cried a lot.		a lot.
12. We copied the papers.		the papers.
13. They blessed the house.		the house.
14. He traveled to Germany.		to Germany.
15. They wrapped the books.		the books.
16. They delayed the plan.		the plan.

H2. Write out the abbreviations.

1. lb   *pound*
2. oz.   _____
3. doz.   _____
4. gal.   _____
5. qt.   _____
6. 1'   _____
7. 2'   _____
8. 1"   _____
9. 2"   _____
10. km.   _____

H3. Write out the numbers.

1. 100   *one hundred*
2. 200   _____
3. 300   _____
4. 400   _____
5. 500   _____
6. 600   _____
7. 700   _____
8. 800   _____
9. 900   _____
10. 120   _____

H4. Write the sentences using contractions.

1. I **do not** buy tomatoes.   *I don't buy tomatoes.*
2. The door **is not** open.   _____
3. Sara **did not** close the door.   _____
4. The box **does not** weigh much.   _____
5. We **are not** students.   _____
6. The children **do not** cry much.   _____
7. They **were not** playing.   _____
8. He **does not** ask questions.   _____
9. Ann **is not** coming today.   _____
10. She **did not** come yesterday.   _____
11. I **was not** working yesterday.   _____
12. Phil and Kathy **are not** friends.   _____

H5. Answer the questions. Follow the example.

1. $5.00 **lb.**

    How much does the **meat** cost?
    *It costs five dollars **a pound.***
    *Please, give me **half a pound** of meat.*

2. $2.00 **gal.**

    How much does the **juice** cost?

    _____

    _____

3. $3.00 **doz.**

    How much do the **eggs** cost?

    _____

    _____

4. $9.00 **oz.**

    How much does the **perfume** cost?

    _____

    _____

5. $4.00 **ea.**

    How much do the **melons** cost?

    _____

    _____

H6. Choose the correct pronunciation of "-ed."

		T	ED	D			T	ED	D
1.	ordered	____	____	X	8.	peeled	____	____	____
2.	drained	____	____	____	9.	added	____	____	____
3.	poured	____	____	____	10.	removed	____	____	____
4.	prepared	____	____	____	11.	blended	____	____	____
5.	tested	____	____	____	12.	carried	____	____	____
6.	toasted	____	____	____	13.	dressed	____	____	____
7.	washed	____	____	____	14.	blessed	____	____	____

H7. Rewrite the story. Change *every year* for *last year*.

Every year Henry **walks** to the lake. Some of his friends **accompany** Henry to the lake. His parents **stay** at home.

Henry **prefers** to buy five pounds of meat. His friends **want** to bring some fish. All **agree** on the salad and the drinks.

When they **arrive** at the lake, they **rest** on the grass. Later they **cross** the lake in a boat and **start** fishing.

There **is** plenty of fish for everybody. Some of the fish **weighs** five pounds.

Others **weigh** half a pound or few ounces. Henry **cooks** the fish. It **tastes** very good.

Last year _____

_____

_____

_____

_____

_____

_____

_____

_____

_____

_____

_____

_____

_____

_____

_____

_____

_____

_____

_____

_____

_____

Lesson #9

Money

Index

Audio & Translations

 English Audio available online for sections A-E.

 Translations in various Languages available online for Sections A, B, and E.

www.BasicESL.com

1. money

2. penny

3. nickel

4. dime

5. quarter

6. 50 cent (*coin*)

7. coins

8. dollar bill

9. stack of money

1. expensive (*ring*)

2. reasonable (*watch*)

3. cheap (*bracelet*)

222

333

444

13. two hundred and twenty-two

14. three hundred and thirty-three

15. four hundred and forty-four

555

666

777

16. five hundred and fifty-five

17. six hundred and sixty-six

18. seven hundred and seventy-seven

16. eight hundred and eighty-eight

17. nine hundred and ninety-nine

18. one thousand

13. two thousand

14. three thousand

15. four thousand

Other Vocabulary

1.	n	worth	**7.**	n	rest	**13.**	v	help
2.	n	week	**8.**	adj	several	**14.**	v	invite
3.	n	loan	**9.**	v	borrow	**15.**	v	lend
4.	n	bank	**10.**	v	cost	**16.**	v	pile
5.	n	vacation	**11.**	v	deposit	**17.**	v	reward
6.	n	garden	**12.**	v	endorse	**18.**	v	save

B1. Regular Verbs: Past Tense: Questions

Henry deposited **two hundred** dollars.
Did Henry deposit **$200**?

Sara needed **three hundred** dollars.
Did Sara need **$300**?

We received **four hundred** dollars.
Did we receive **$400**?

The family saved **five hundred** dollars.
Did the family save **$500**?

B2. Regular Verbs: Past Tense: Questions

He endorsed the check for **six hundred** dollars.
Did he endorse the check for **$600**?

You borrowed **seven hundred** dollars.
Did you borrow **$700**?

They changed **eight hundred** dollars.
Did they change **$800**?

She piled up **one thousand** dollars in debt.
Did she pile up **$1,000** in debt?

B3. Regular Verbs: Past Tense: Questions and Answers

Did Mike **stop** coming?
   Yes, he stopp**ed** coming.
   No, he **didn't stop** coming.

Did the sack **weigh** a lot?
   Yes, it weigh**ed** a lot.
   No, it **didn't weigh** a lot.

Did she **cry** at night?
   Yes, she **cr**i**ed** at night.
   No, she **didn't cry** at night.

B1 - B2 - B3 - B4

Questions in the *past tense* are formed with the word *"did"* at the beginning of the question.

*The form of the verb is the **base form** and it is **the same** for all subjects. In questions we do not add **"-ed"** to the form of the verb.*

B4. Regular Verbs: Past Tense: Questions and Answers

B1 - B4 (continued)

Did you **climb** the mountain?
Yes, I climb**ed** the mountain.
No, I **did not climb** the mountain.

Did he **stay** there long?
Yes, he stay**ed** there long.
No, he **didn't stay** there long.

Did they **help** John?
Yes, they help**ed** John.
No, they **didn't help** John.

B5. Question Words: Money

How much is a **dollar** worth?
It is worth 100 cents.

How much is a **quarter** worth?
It is worth 25 cents.

How much is a **dime** worth?
It is worth 10 cents.

How much is a **nickel** worth?
It is worth 5 cents.

B6. Question Words: Money

How many quarters are there in a dollar?
There are **four** quarters.

How many nickels are there in a dollar?
There are **twenty** nickels.

How many dimes are there in a dollar?
There are **ten** dimes in a dollar.

How many pennies are there in a quarter?
There are **twenty-five** pennies in a quarter.

C1. Read and Listen to the story.

Every week Carl **helps** his dad in the garden. His father **rewards** his son with a twenty dollar bill. Carl **is** very happy. He **plans** to save enough money to buy a bicycle. Last year he **saved** a lot of money.

As soon as Carl **receives** the money from his father, he **walks** to the bank and **changes** the 20 dollar bill for a ten dollar bill, a five dollar bill and several coins: twelve quarters, ten dimes and one hundred pennies.

Every week Carl **saves** the ten dollar bill for his bicycle. His cousin **borrows** the five dollar bill and **deposits** the bill in the bank. With the rest of the money, Carl **invites** his friends to an ice cream.

C2. Listening Exercise: Listen to the story.

Last week Carl **helped** his dad in the garden. His father **rewarded** his son with a twenty dollar bill. Carl **was** very happy. He **planned** to save enough money to buy a bicycle. Last year he **saved** a lot of money.

As soon as Carl **received** the money from his father, he **walked** to the bank and **changed** the 20 dollar bill for a ten dollar bill, a five dollar bill and several coins: twelve quarters, ten dimes and one hundred pennies.

Last week Carl **saved** the ten dollar bill for his bicycle. His cousin **borrowed** the five dollar bill and **deposited** the bill in the bank. With the rest of the money, Carl **invited** his friends to an ice cream.

D1. worth / how many

What is this?
This is a penny.

How much is a penny worth?
It is worth one cent.

How many pennies are in one dollar?
There are **100** pennies in one dollar.

D2. worth / how many

What is this?
This is a nickel.

How much is a nickel worth?
It is worth five cents.

How many nickels are in one dollar?
There are **twenty** nickels in one dollar.

D3. worth / how many

What is this?
This is a dime.

How much is a dime worth?
It is worth ten cents.

How many dimes are in one dollar?
There are **ten** dimes in one dollar.

D4. worth / how many

What is this?
This is a quarter.

How much is a quarter worth?
It is worth twenty-five cents.

How many quarters are in one dollar?
There are **four** quarters in one dollar.

Asking for a favor.

1. Excuse me, can I ask you a question?
2. *Yes, of course.*
3. Can I borrow your pen?
4. I have to fill out a form.
5. *Here it is.*
6. Thank you very much.
7. *Don't mention it.*
8. *Listen, I'm in a hurry.*
9. *You can keep the pen.*
10. This is very nice of you.

For the English audio pronunciations and written native language translations of **section E,** please go to:

www.basicesl.com

Excuse me, can I ask a question?

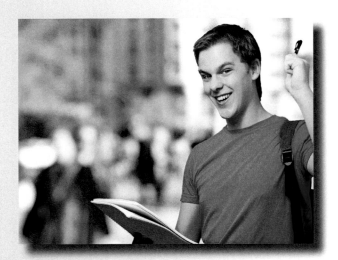

Thank you very much.

End of the **oral exercises** for lesson 9.
You can find additional exercises in sections D, F & G at Basic ESL Online.

Please continue with the **written exercises** for this lesson in **section H**.

Lesson

9

H1. Change the sentence to a question. Answer the question.

1. He **carried** the sack.

    Did he **carry** the sack?

    *Yes, he **carried** the sack.*

    *No, he **did not carry** the sack.*

2. She endorsed the checks.

    _____

    _____

    _____

3. Ann copied the letter.

    _____

    _____

    _____

4. She stopped at the store.

    _____

    _____

    _____

5. She fried the fish.

    _____

    _____

    _____

H2. Answer the question.

1. 33 **lb.**   How much **sugar** does he buy?
*He buys **thirty-three** pounds of sugar.*

2. 22 **gal.**   How much **juice** did they want?

_____

3. 44 **doz.**   How many **eggs** did the church purchase?

_____

4. $0.55 **oz.**   How much does the **perfume** cost?

_____

5. 66 **ea.**   How many **gold coins** did the children receive?

_____

6. 77 **kg.**   How much **weight** did Harold gain?

_____

H3. Answer the questions.

Question	Answer
1. Did you want the pen?	Yes, *I **wanted** the pen.*
	No, *I **didn't want** the pen.*
2. Do they agree to this?	Yes, _____
	No, _____
3. Did Mary invite John?	Yes, _____
	No, _____
4. Does he recognize Sara?	Yes, _____
	No, _____
5. Did you attempt to leave?	Yes, _____
	No, _____

H4. Answer the questions.

1. Are **the boys** tall?   *Yes, **they** are tall.*
2. Does **Mary** learn English?   *Yes, **she** learns English.*
3. Did Mary learn German?
4. Does Mary study music?
5. Did Mary study Russian?
6. Did Tom purchase books?
7. Does Tom like pencils?
8. Were the vegetables fresh?
9. Does Ann use a pen?
10. Did she want a desk?
11. Does she want a lamp?
12. Does she need a flag?
13. Did you need a chair?
14. Was Joe looking for bread?
15. Was the bread good?
16. Do I have a big family?
17. Did you use any salt?
18. Did Tom play at home?
19. Does he play at school?
20. Did Mary complain a lot?
21. Does she complain often?
22. Is she complaining now?
23. Did you like the desk?
24. Does Mary enjoy the class?
25. Did Carol listen to Jane?
26. Are you living in France?

H5. Follow the example.

1.

penny

How **much** is a penny worth?
   It is worth one cent.

How **many** pennies are there in one dollar?
   There are one hundred pennies in a dollar.

2.

nickel

3.

dime

4.

quarter

Chapter 4

Location, Order & Manner

Lesson 10:   Location
Lesson 11:   Order
Lesson 12:   Shapes & Manner

What to do in each section of every lesson...

A - Vocabulary Study

Section A includes the vocabulary that will be used throughout the lesson. Learning new vocabulary is basic to learning a new language.

Read the vocabulary several times.
If you are on Basic ESL Online:
Listen to the **English audio pronunciation**.
View the **native language translations** of the vocabulary.

Listen and read the vocabulary until you can understand the vocabulary without looking at the words.

B - Sentence Structure

Section B teaches students basic English sentences using the vocabulary in section A.

Read and **study** the sentences.
If you are on Basic ESL Online:
Listen to the **English audio pronunciation**.
View the **native language translations** of the sentences.
View the **grammar concepts** by clicking on the **information button** 🛈 .

Repeat the sentences as many times as needed. Continue to the next section once you can **understand** the sentences without looking at them.

C - Listening Exercises

Read the story or dialog several times.
If you are on Basic ESL Online, **listen** to the story or dialog while reading it several times.

Once you are familiar with the story or dialog, try to see if you can **understand** it by only listening without reading.

D - Conversation Exercises

Read the conversation dialogs several times.
If you are on Basic ESL Online, **listen** to the dialogs until you can understand them without looking at them.

Finally, try to **speak** the conversation dialogs by only looking at the pictures and key words.

E - Common Phrases

Many of the **common phrases** that are presented in this section are frequently used by the native English speakers in their everyday life.

Read the common phrases several times.
If you are on Basic ESL Online, **listen** to the common phrases while reading. **Listen** as many times as needed until you can understand the common phrases without looking at the sentences.

H - Written Exercises

The written exercises provide an opportunity to test what you learned in the lesson. You can never be sure of knowing something unless you can put it in writing.

You can check your answers by going to the **Answer Key Section** in the back of the workbook.

For information regarding **Basic ESL Online,** please visit **www.basicesl.com**.
🎧 Audio Pronunciaton of English & 📖 Native Language Translations.

Lesson #10

Location

Index

Audio & Translations

English Audio available online for sections A-E.

Translations in various Languages available online for Sections A, B, and E.

www.BasicESL.com

1. above (*the water*)

2. in the middle

3. below (*the woman*)

4. in (*the box*)

5. outside (*the tent*)

6. inside (*the hole*)

7. on top of (*the building*)

8. under (*the table*)

9. through (*the needle*)

10. over (*the mountain*)

11. behind (*the fence*)

12. around (*the tree*)

13. by (*the fire*)

14. in front of (*the car*)

15. among (*the fruit*)

16. against (*the wall*)

17. between (*the girls*)

18. upside down

19. up (*the hill*)   **20.** down (*the hill*)   **21.** to (*the right*)

Other Vocabulary

1.	n	bookcase	**10.**	v	catch
2.	n	bottom	**11.**	v	nail
3.	n	speech	**12.**	v	convince
4.	n	nothing	**13.**	v	hear
5.	n	vase	**14.**	v	shoot
6.	n	nail	**15.**	v	succeed
7.	adj	broad	**16.**	v	support
8.	v	cause	**17.**	v	see
9.	v	drive	**18.**	pre	at

For the audio pronunciations and written translations of **Sections A and B,** please go to:

www.basicesl.com

Looking for Bilingual Dictionaries?
You can find a large selection at:

www.bilingualdictionaries.com

B1. Modal Verb "can-could": Ability

I **can** walk.
I **am able** to walk.

You **can** lift this box.
You **are able** to lift this box.

He **could** eat a little.
He **was able** to eat a little.

She **could** open her eyes.
She **was able** to open her eyes.

B2. Modal Verb "can-could": Negative Sentences

I **cannot** walk.
I **can't** walk.
I **am not able** to walk.

You **cannot** lift this box.
You **can't** lift this box.
You **are not able** to lift this box.

You **could not** eat much.
You **couldn't** eat much.
You **were not able** to eat much.

B3. Modal Verb "can-could": Negative Sentences

She **could not** open her eyes.
She **couldn't** open her eyes.
She **was not able** to open her eyes.

We **could not** sleep last night.
We **couldn't** sleep last night.
We **were not able** to sleep last night.

They **cannot** chew.
They **can't** chew
They **are not able** to chew.

B1 - B4

Modal verbs are those auxiliary verbs used to express different attitudes of the subject regarding the action of the verb. These attitudes of the subject can express: **advise, ability, obligation, permission, necessity, decision** or **probability.** They are followed by the main verb without **"to."** The form of the verb is the same for all subjects.

The modal verb **can** (present tense) and **could** (past tense) express meanings of **permission, possibility, request** or **ability.** When expressing ability we can also use the verb **"to be able."** The negative forms are: **"cannot (can't)"** and **"could not (couldn't)."**

B4. Modal Verb "can-could": Possibility

I cannot do it now.
I **could** do it tomorrow.

She can't come today.
She **could** come tomorrow.

They cannot accuse Mary.
They **could** accuse Tom.

We can't say yes now.
We **could** say yes tomorrow.

B1-B4 (continued)

B5. Modal Verb "can-could": Requests

Can I borrow a pen?
    Yes, you **can** borrow a pen.
    No, you **cannot** borrow a pen.

Can I ask a question?
    Yes, you **can** ask a question.
    No, you **cannot** ask a question.

Can I make a call?
    Yes, you **can** make a call.
    No, you **cannot** make a call.

B5

Questions with modal verbs are formed with the verb "can" or "could" at the beginning of the question.

B6. Modal Verb "can-could": Short Answers

Can I sit down now?
Yes, you **can**.
No, you **can't**.

Can he go to the bathroom?
Yes, he **can**.
No, he **can't**.

Could they speak to the President?
Yes, they **could**.
No, they **couldn't**.

C1. Read and Listen to the story.

Mr. Finch works **in** an office at home. One can see **in** the office: a table, several pictures, a book-case, a chair and a pair of shoes **under** the chair.

Regarding the pictures, Mr. Finch does not hang pictures **on** the wall. He nails the pictures **to** the wall. There is a big picture **between** the windows. There is a lamp **above** the big picture, and there is nothing **below** the picture.

Mr. Finch has a vase **with** flowers **on top of** the bookcase. He puts the small books **on** the top shelf. There are some small family pictures **on** the middle shelf.

C2. Read and Listen to the story.

Every day my **mom prepares** the main meal. **She starts** with the soup. **She makes** her favorite pea soup. **She washes** the peas and **boils** the soup on the stove.

While the soup is boiling, **she prepares** the main course of meat with onions. **She trims** the fat from the meat and **sprinkles** the meat with a little salt. **She chops** an onion and **fries** the meat with onions.

For dessert **she prepares** a fruit salad. **She splits** a melon, **peels** an orange and **cuts** a banana. Finally, **she mixes** the orange, the melon and the banana together.

D1. man / car

What do you see in this picture?
I see a man and a car.

Where is the man?
He is **in front** of the car.

Where is the car?
It is **behind** the man.

D2. red dot / yellow

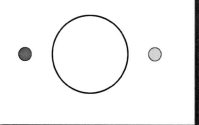

What do you see in this picture?
I see a red dot and a yellow one.

Where is the red dot?
It is **to the left** of the circle.

Where is the yellow dot?
It is **to the right** of the circle.

D3. dot / circle

What do you see in this picture?
I see one dot and a circle.

Where is the dot?
It is **above** the circle.

Where is the circle?
It's **below** the dot.

D4. purple dot / gray

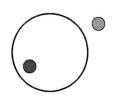

What do you see in this picture?
I see a purple dot and a gray one.

Where is the purple dot?
It's **inside** the circle.

Where is the gray one?
It's **outside** the circle.

Bad News

1. You look sad. What's wrong?
2. *My uncle passed away.*
3. I am sorry to hear that.
4. What happened?
5. *He died suddenly yesterday.*
6. Was it a heart attack?
7. *I don't believe so.*
8. What else could it be?
9. *I wish I knew.*
10. *The doctor doesn't know either.*

For the English audio pronunciations and written native language translations of **section E,** please go to:

www.basicesl.com

You look sad. What's wrong?

What else could it be?

End of the **oral exercises** for lesson 10.

You can find additional exercises in sections D, F & G at Basic ESL Online.

Please continue with the **written exercises** for this lesson in **section H**.

Lesson
10

H1. Make the sentence negative.

1. I **can** work.   *I **cannot** (can't) work.*
2. He **can** see you.   _____
3. We **can** walk.   _____
4. You **can** go.   _____
5. She **can** say this.   _____
6. They **can** travel.   _____
7. Sara **can** cook.   _____

H2. Make the sentence negative.

1. They **could** hear.   *They **could not** (couldn't) hear.*
2. He **could** see.   _____
3. We **could** walk.   _____
4. You **could** go.   _____
5. She **could** fly.   _____
6. They **could** travel.   _____
7. Sara **could** cook.   _____

H3. Change the statements to questions.

Statement	Question
1. They **could** hear the noise.	*Could* they hear the noise?
2. He **can** walk now.	
3. We **can** talk to Peter.	
4. You **can** go by plane.	
5. He **could** fly to France.	
6. They **can** travel by car.	
7. Sara **could** succeed.	
8. Mike **can** play two hours.	
9. Fred **could** study at night.	
10. We **can** write letters.	

H4. Answer the questions.

Question	Long Answer	Short Answer
1. **Can** Susan drive?	*Yes*, she **can** drive. *No*, she **cannot** drive.	*Yes, she* **can.** *No, she* **can't.**
2. **Can** the children walk?		
3. **Can** Henry do that?		
4. **Can** I help Mary?		
5. **Could** they talk?		

H5. Complete with any of these prepositions: *on, in, to, at*

1. Tom is ___ the classroom.	*in*	11. Look ___ that picture.	_____
2. I am not ___ home.	_____	12. The picture is ___ the wall.	_____
3. I am ___ the school.	_____	13. My father is ___ the office.	_____
4. Move ___ the right.	_____	14. Tom is ___ the roof.	_____
5. She is ___ the gymnasium.	_____	15. My sister is ___ the attic.	_____
6. Listen ___ the teacher.	_____	16. Frank is ___ the porch.	_____
7. Open the book ___ page 2.	_____	17. I am ___ the middle.	_____
8. We go ___ bed early.	_____	18. We go ___ bed early.	_____
9. The store is ___ the corner.	_____	19. It is ___ the back of the car.	_____
10. The books are ___ the shelf.	_____	20. The flag is ___ top of the desk.	_____

H6. Make the statements *negative*. Change the **bold** words *opposite*.

1. Stay **in front of** the fence.   *Don't stay **behind** the fence.*

2. Go **down** the hill. _____

3. Turn **right**. _____

4. Put the book **on** the desk. _____

5. Write **above** the line. _____

6. Stay **outside** the house. _____

7. Put the vase **under** the table _____

8. Keep the child **far** from Fred. _____

9. Sit **away** from the fire. _____

10. Keep the shoes **in** the box. _____

H7. Follow the example.

1.   dot / circle

What do you see in this picture?
     *I see a **dot** and a **circle**.*

Where is the dot?
     *It is **on top** of the circle.*

Where is the circle?
     *It is **under** the dot.*

2.   dot / circle

_____

_____

_____

_____

_____

_____

3.   girl / desk

_____

_____

_____

_____

_____

_____

4.   thread / girl

_____

_____

_____

_____

_____

_____

Lesson #11

Order

Index

Audio & Translations

English Audio available online for sections A-E.

Translations in various Languages available online for Sections A, B, and E.

www.BasicESL.com

1. first

2. one

3. second

4. two

5. third

6. three

7. fourth

8. four

9. fifth

5

10. five

6ᵗʰ

11. sixth

6

12. six

7ᵗʰ

13. seventh

7

14. seven

8ᵗʰ

15. eighth

8

16. eight

9ᵗʰ

17. ninth

9

18. nine

10th	**11**th	**12**th
19. tenth	**20.** eleventh	**21.** twelfth

Other Vocabulary

1.	n	gift	**10.**	v	attack
2.	adj	alive	**11.**	v	allow
3.	adj	ashamed	**12.**	v	claim
4.	adj	blond	**13.**	v	fail
5.	adj	bored	**14.**	v	feed
6.	adj	clever	**15.**	v	improve
7.	adj	nasty	**16.**	v	believe
8.	adj	stupid	**17.**	v	underline
9.	adj	usual	**18.**	v	expect

For the audio pronunciations and written translations of **Sections A and B,** please go to:

www.basicesl.com

B1. Ordinal Numbers

1st	This is my **first** pen.	
2nd	Ann is my **second** child.	
3rd	The **third** book is thick.	
4th	My **fourth** year was hard.	
5th	The **fifth** ticket was free.	
6th	Sit on the **sixth** chair.	
7th	This is the **seventh** time.	
8th	You're the **eighth** in line.	
9th	The **ninth** day was bad.	
10th	The **tenth** day was good.	

B2. Ordinal and Cardinal Numbers

We were **eight** children in class.
I was sitting in the **eighth** row.

Who was the **next to the last**?
Anne was the **next to the last**.

Do you have **two** brothers?
No, the **second** one is dead.

Who feeds the **five** children?
The **fifth** one is hungry.

B3. Ordinal and Cardinal Numbers

There was **one** girl in line
She was the **first** one.

I have **three** brothers.
The **third** brother was sick.

We prepared **four** lessons.
The **fourth** lesson was very easy.

You tried **six** times.
The **sixth** time you succeeded.

B1 - B2 - B3

Ordinal numbers are used to indicate **order**. As a rule, they are formed by adding *"-th"* to the cardinal number. *Cardinal numbers* are used to **count** people or objects.

B4. Verbs: Past Tense: Short Answers

Did you **fail** in English?
Yes, I **did**.
No, I **didn't**.

Did Ann **improve** her grades?
Yes, she **did**.
No, she **didn't**.

Did I **say** that? I don't remember.
Yes, you **did**.
No, you **didn't**.

B4 - B5

*A **short answer** in the past tense consists of the **subject** followed by "did" or "did not (didn't)."*

B5. Verbs: Past Tense: Short Answers

Did it **happen** fast?
Yes, it **did**.
No, it **didn't**.

Did I **arrive** late?
Yes, you **did**.
No, you **didn't**.

Did Peter **catch** a cold?
Yes, he **did**.
No, he **didn't**.

B6. Question Words About Measurements

What was the width of the door?
How wide was the door?

What was your height before?
How tall were you?

What is the thickness of the book?
How thick is the book?

What is the depth of the river?
How deep is the river?

B6 (Review)

C - Reading and Listening 11-7

C1. Read and Listen to the dialog.

*Where does Mr. Finch work **at** home?*
    He works **in** an office.

*Do you see a chair **by** the fireplace?*
    No, I don't see any chair **by** the fireplace.

*What is there **under** his chair?*
    It is a pair **of** shoes.

*How many pictures are there **on** the wall?*
    There is only one big picture **on** the wall.

Where is the big picture?
    It is **between** the windows.

C2. Read and Listen to the dialog.

*What is **above** the picture?*
    A lamp is **above** the picture.

*Do you see a lamp **below** the picture?*
    No, I don't. There is nothing there.

*Is there a lamp **over** his desk?*
    No, there is a lamp **on** his desk.

*What's **on top of** the bookcase?*
    There is a vase **with** flowers.

Where does he put his family pictures?
    He puts the pictures **in** the middle shelf.

D1. 1ˢᵗ / 24" x 80"/ size

What do you see in the first picture?
I see a door in the first picture.

How many doors do you see?
I see one door in the first picture.

What's the size of the door?
It's 24" wide x 80" long.

D2. 2ⁿᵈ / 4" / size

What do you see in the second picture?
I see sandwiches in the second picture.

How many sandwiches do you see?
I see two sandwiches in the second picture.

What size are the sandwiches?
They're 4" thick.

D3. 3ʳᵈ / regular / size

What do you see in the third picture?
I see hamburgers.

How many hamburgers do you see?
I see three hamburgers in the third picture.

What size are the hamburgers?
They are a regular size.

D4. 4ᵗʰ / teaspoons / size

What do you see in the fourth picture?
I see spoons in the fourth picture.

How many spoons do you see?
I see four spoons in the fourth picture.

What size are the spoons?
They're teaspoons.

Making excuses

1. **Do you want to go to the beach?**
2. *I'm sorry. I have other plans.*
3. *I'm not going to be able.*
4. *I have an appointment.*
5. *Today is a bad day for me.*
6. **How about next week?**
7. *Let me check my schedule.*
8. *I am busy on Saturday.*
9. **How about next Sunday?**
10. *That is okay. See you soon.*

For the English audio pronunciations and written native language translations of **section E,** please go to:

www.basicesl.com

Do you want to go to the beach?

How about next Saturday?

End of the **oral exercises** for lesson 11.
You can find additional exercises in sections D, F & G at Basic ESL Online.

Please continue with the **written exercises** for this lesson in **section H**.

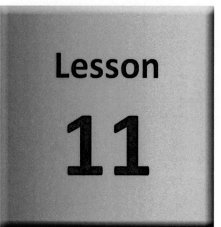

Lesson

11

H1. Write these numbers.

Cardinal Numbers		Ordinal Numbers	
1.	*one*	1st	*first*
2.	_____	2nd	_____
3.	_____	3rd	_____
4.	_____	4th	_____
5.	_____	5th	_____
6.	_____	6th	_____
7.	_____	7th	_____
8.	_____	8th	_____
9.	_____	9th	_____
10.	_____	10th	_____

H2. Write the name of these states.

1.	FL	*Florida*	7.	NY	_____
2.	TX	_____	8.	WI	_____
3.	CA	_____	9.	IL	_____
4.	CO	_____	10.	AL	_____
5.	AZ	_____	11.	WA	_____
6.	NM	_____	12.	OR	_____

H3. Answer with short answers.

1. Did they improve their grades? *Yes, they did.* *No, they didn't.*
2. Did you fail the test?
3. Did Liz underline that word?
4. Did Mrs. Rice allow that?
5. Did the dog attack Greg?
6. Did the ladies feed the poor?
7. Did you do it?

H4. Answer with short answers.

1. Does Tom expect to win? *Yes, he does.* *No, he doesn't.*
2. Are there any doubts?
3. Do you believe Carol?
4. Were you sure of that?
5. Does the school have TV?
6. Is there any other question?
7. Was Mary far away?

H5. Make correct sentences.

1. be-yesterday-there- you? *Were you there yesterday?*
2. cross-they-yesterday-street?
3. he-work-today-be?
4. you-for-study-test-always?
5. you-what-see-picture?
6. questions-answer-all-Mary?
7. peel-Smith-tomatoes-Mrs.

H6. Follow the example.

1.   5th / green / dot

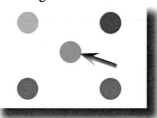

What do you see in the fifth picture?
    I see several dots.

How many dots do you see?
    I see five dots in the fifth picture.

Where is the green dot?
    It is in the center.

2.   6th / red / star

_____

_____

_____

_____

_____

_____

3.   7th / 9"

_____

_____

_____

_____

_____

_____

4.   8th / .025 ea

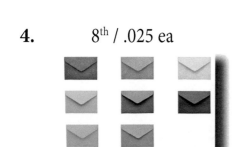

_____

_____

_____

_____

_____

_____

_____

H7. Follow the example.

1. you

   Tampa, FL

   345 3rd Ave.

   Where did you use to live?
   I used to live in Tampa, Florida.

   What was your address?
   My address was three hundred forty-five 3rd Ave.

2. Paul

   Chicago, IL

   806 11th St.

   _____

   _____

   _____

   _____

   _____

3. parents

   Dallas, TX

   227 4th Ave.

   _____

   _____

   _____

   _____

   _____

4. Liz

   Salem, OR

   589 6th Ave.

   _____

   _____

   _____

   _____

   _____

Lesson #12

Shapes & Manner

Audio & Translations

English Audio available online for sections A-E.

Translations in various Languages available online for Sections A, B, and E.

www.BasicESL.com

1. round

2. circle

3. cube

4. oval

5. rectangle

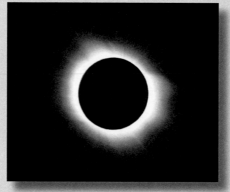

6. square

7. cylinder

8. triangle

9. pentagon

10. sphere

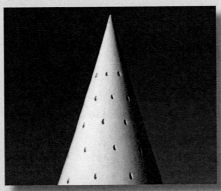

11. cone

12. globe

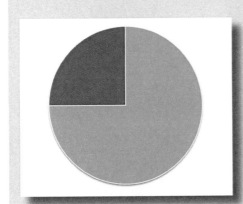

13. one fourth

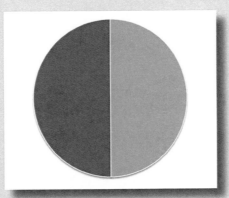

14. half

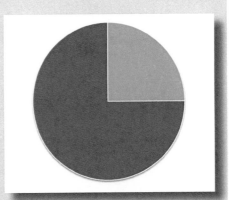

15. three fourths

16. whole

17. horizontal

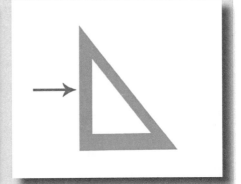

18. vertical

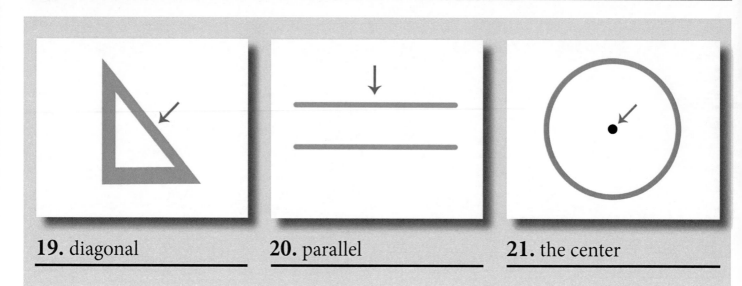

19. diagonal   **20.** parallel   **21.** the center

13. circumference   **14.** the radius   **15.** the angle

Other Vocabulary

1.	n	cook	**7.**	adj	important	**13.**	v	challenge
2.	n	driver	**8.**	adj	loud	**14.**	v	chase
3.	n	singer	**9.**	adj	slow	**15.**	v	crash
4.	n	waitress	**10.**	adj	true	**16.**	v	crush
5.	adj	clear	**11.**	v	arrest	**17.**	v	delay
6.	adj	false	**12.**	v	beg	**18.**	v	throw

B1. Adverbs of Manner

adj	Mike is a **slow** player.
adv	He plays slow**ly**.
adj	Pat is a **careful** driver.
adv	She drives careful**ly**.
adj	Fred is a **serious** person.
adv	He speaks very serious**ly**.
adj	Tony is not a **bad** boy.
adv	He does not behave bad**ly**.

B1

Adverbs *are words that describe verbs.* *Adverbs of manner* *indicate* **how** *the action of the verb is done.*

B2. Adverbs of Manner

adj	He is a **strong** boxer.
adv	He hits strong**ly**.
adj	You are **polite**.
adv	You speak polite**ly**.
adj	Henry speaks in a **loud** voice.
adv	Henry speaks loud**ly**.
adj	The course is a **quick** course.
adv	You finished the course quick**ly**.

B2

Most adverbs of manner are formed by adding "-ly" to the adjective.

B3. Adjectives ending in "-y" and "-ble"

adj	These lessons are e**asy**.
adv	Ray learns the lessons easi**ly**.
adj	The boys are **happy**.
adv	They play happi**ly**.
adj	The girls are **responsible**.
adv	They act responsib**ly**.
adj	This theory is **probable**.
adv	The theory is probab**ly** correct.

B3

For adjectives ending in "-y", change the "-y" to i before adding "-ly."

Adjectives ending in "-ble" drop the "-e" before adding "-ly."

B4. Adverbs of Manner: Irregular Forms

B4

adj	She is a **good** teacher.
adv	She teaches **well**.
adj	Paul is a **hard** worker.
adv	He works **hard**.
adj	Liz is a **fast** runner.
adv	She runs very **fast**.

Irregular adverbs of manner do not add "-ly" to the form of the adjective.

The following are irregular adverbs of manner: "good, hard and fast."

B5. Similar Adjectives: "like, same, similar"

What is your shirt **like**?
It is **like** your shirt.
I **like** your shirt.
It is **unlike** any other.

It is not **the same as** mine.
It is **similar to** mine.
But it is **different from** mine.
We are not going to look **alike**.
It is very **unlikely**.

B6. Question Words: Measurements

B6 (Review)

What is the wealth of Peter?
How wealthy is Peter?

What size is the table?
How large (big) is the table?

What is the **thinness** of the pen?
How thin is the pen?

What is the **height** of the mountain?
How high is the mountain?

C1. Read and Listen to the Story.

Last year Mr. Finch **worked** in an office at home. One **could** see a table, several pictures, a bookcase, a chair and a pair of shoes under the chair.

Regarding the pictures, Mr. Finch **nailed** the pictures to the wall. There **was** a big picture between the windows. There **was** a lamp above the big picture, and there **was nothing** below the picture.

Mr. Finch **placed** a vase with flowers on top of the bookcase. There **were** some small family pictures on the middle shelf. His heavy books **were** at the bottom of the bookcase.

C2. Read and Listen to the Story.

My three sisters eat two meals at home. Before going to school they eat a light breakfast: a glass of orange juice and a bowl of cereal. Our parents have a cup of coffee and a piece of toast with marmalade. When there is no milk they drink water.

Today there is no juice in the refrigerator. There are only two bottles of milk. There are no boxes of cereals in the pantry. Also, there is no jar of marmalade. This is why my sisters are eating ham and eggs today. Instead of a light breakfast, they are having a full breakfast.

D1. Ann / to drive / careful / 17

Ann is driving the car.
She is a careful driver.

How old is she?
    She is only seventeen.

How carefully does she drive?
    She drives very carefully.

D2. Carol / to serve / fast / 18

Carol is serving the tables.
She is a fast waitress.

How old is she?
    She is only eighteen.

How fast does she serve?
    She serves the tables very fast.

D3. Mary / to sing / good / 15

Mary is singing on the stage.
She is a good singer.

How old is she?
    She is only fifteen years old.

How well does she sing?
    She sings very well.

D4. Tom-Mike / to cook / bad / 30

Tom and Mike are cooking today.
They are bad cooks.

How old are they?
    They are 30 years old.

How badly do they cook?
    They cook very badly.

Expressing pain

1. My throat hurts.
2. My neck hurts.
3. I feel pain in the arm.
4. I feel pain in the leg.
5. I feel like vomiting.
6. I feel dizzy.
7. This finger is bothering me.
8. I have a headache.
9. I have a stomach ache.
10. I have a toothache.

For the English audio pronunciations and written native language translations of **section E,** please go to:

www.basicesl.com

My throat hurts.

I feel pain in my arm.

End of the **oral exercises** for lesson 12.
You can find additional exercises in sections D, F & G at Basic ESL Online.

Please continue with the **written exercises** for this lesson in **section H**.

Lesson
12

H1. Form adverbs of manner.

1. clear   *slowly*
2. strong _____
3. brave _____
4. careful _____
5. bad _____
6. polite _____

7. full _____
8. easy _____
9. good _____
10. happy _____
11. fast _____
12. probable _____

H2. Is it an adjective or and adverb?

	Adjective	Adverb
1. He's a **polite** boy.	X	_____
2. She writes **correctly**.	_____	_____
3. The answer is **clear**.	_____	_____
4. The boy is **strong**.	_____	_____
5. It's an **easy** lesson.	_____	_____
6. We drive **slowly**.	_____	_____
7. I have **deep** emotions.	_____	_____
8. I am **deeply** sorry.	_____	_____

H3. Complete with adjectives or adverbs.

1. **bad**   Joe and Ray are ___ boys.   *bad*

   They behave very ___ .   *badly*

2. **easy**   Lesson 5 is not ___ .   _____

   One cannot learn this lesson ___ .   _____

3. **happy**   Are you ___ in your new house?   _____

   Yes, we're living ___ there.   _____

4. **slow**   Try to avoid the ___ driver.   _____

   Fred is driving very ___ .   _____

5. **strong**   You pushed Mike ___ .   _____

   Mike is not too ___ .   _____

6. **quick**   Can you answer more ___ ?   _____

   Don't make ___ decisions.   _____

7. **good**   You have very ___ grades.   _____

   Did you study ___ for the test?   _____

8. **careful**   We are very ___ men.   _____

   We do things ___ .   _____

H4. Read the story and answer the questions.

This year Mr. Finch has an office at home. There are several things in it: a table, a chair, two pictures and a bookcase. The table is big and old. I don't know its exact measurements. It is about 60" long by 30" wide.

A chair is behind the table. There are two pictures on the wall. Mr. Finch does not hang the pictures. He nails the pictures to the wall.

The big picture is in the middle of the wall, between two lamps. Its width is 20" only, but its length is almost 5'. The small picture is above the bookcase.

The bookcase is 36" wide, 100" long, and 18" deep. The top shelf holds the thin books. He keeps the thick books on the bottom shelf. There are no books in the middle shelf. He keeps the family pictures there.

Answer the questions.

1. What is the table like in the office of Mr. Finch?

2. Is there anything behind the table?

3. How many pictures are there on the wall?

4. What is the size of the big picture?

5. Does he hang the pictures on the wall?

6. Where does he keep the small family pictures?

H5. Choose the correct answer.

1. Circle the cardinal numbers.	one	second	third	fourth
2. Underline the first word.	home	pie	weight	pint
3. Cross out the third word.	circle	wall	box	shelf
4. I sit in the ___ row.	two	sixth	six	sixteen
5. A word with a question mark.	girl's;	who?	excellent!	"ice-cream"
6. Circle the adverb.	bad	good	well	careful

H6. Multiple choice: Choose the correct answer.

1. He poured some juice _____ the cup.   **in**, at, on, of, for
2. The two boys are playing _____ home.   in, at, on, of, for
3. The box_____ oranges isn't heavy.   in, at, on, of, for
4. Don't put that box _____ the floor.   in, at, on, of, for
5. I waited _____ Jane at school.   in, at, on, of, for
6. _____Fred borrowed some money yesterday?   Does, Do, Did, Can
7. I can't lift the box _____ .   easy, easily, heavily
8. It isn't _____ to lift the box.   easy, easily, heavily
9. He doesn't write very _____ .   good, far, well
10. What's your father _____ ?   nice, like, tall, heavy

Chapter 5

Animals

Lesson 13:   Domestic Animals
Lesson 14:   Wild Animals
Lesson 15:   Other Animals

What to do in each section of every lesson...

A - Vocabulary Study

Section A includes the vocabulary that will be used throughout the lesson. Learning new vocabulary is basic to learning a new language.

Read the vocabulary several times.
If you are on Basic ESL Online:
Listen to the **English audio pronunciation**.
View the **native language translations** of the vocabulary.

Listen and read the vocabulary until you can understand the vocabulary without looking at the words.

B - Sentence Structure

Section B teaches students basic English sentences using the vocabulary in section A.

Read and **study** the sentences.
If you are on Basic ESL Online:
Listen to the **English audio pronunciation**.
View the **native language translations** of the sentences.
View the **grammar concepts** by clicking on the **information button** .

Repeat the sentences as many times as needed. Continue to the next section once you can **understand** the sentences without looking at them.

C - Listening Exercises

Read the story or dialog several times.
If you are on Basic ESL Online, **listen** to the story or dialog while reading it several times.

Once you are familiar with the story or dialog, try to see if you can **understand** it by only listening without reading.

D - Conversation Exercises

Read the conversation dialogs several times.
If you are on Basic ESL Online, **listen** to the dialogs until you can understand them without looking at them.

Finally, try to **speak** the conversation dialogs by only looking at the pictures and key words.

E - Common Phrases

Many of the **common phrases** that are presented in this section are frequently used by the native English speakers in their everyday life.

Read the common phrases several times.
If you are on Basic ESL Online, **listen** to the common phrases while reading. **Listen** as many times as needed until you can understand the common phrases without looking at the sentences.

H - Written Exercises

The written exercises provide an opportunity to test what you learned in the lesson. You can never be sure of knowing something unless you can put it in writing.

You can check your answers by going to the **Answer Key Section** in the back of the workbook.

For information regarding **Basic ESL Online**, please visit **www.basicesl.com**.
 Audio Pronunciaton of English & Native Language Translations.

Lesson #13

Domestic Animals

Index

Audio & Translations

English Audio available online for sections A-E.

Translations in various Languages available online for Sections A, B, and E.

www.BasicESL.com

1. cow

2. sheep

3. ox

4. chicken

5. horse

6. camel

7. cat

8. dog

9. rabbit

10. donkey

11. goose

12. duck

13. calf

14. turkey

15. chick

16. cub

17. deer

18. hamster

19. hare

20. peacock

21. pigeon

22. pig

23. puppy

24. rooster

Other Vocabulary

1.	n	farm	**7.**	adj	frightened	**13.**	v	run
2.	adj	common	**8.**	adj	lucky	**14.**	v	spend
3.	adj	countless	**9.**	adj	sticky	**15.**	v	act
4.	adj	eager	**10.**	adj	violent	**16.**	adv	most
5.	adj	fierce	**11.**	adj	worried	**17.**	con	unless
6.	adj	free	**12.**	v	belong	**18.**	adv	until

B1. Possessive Adjectives and Pronouns

ℹ️

	Possessive **Adjectives**	Possessive **Pronouns**
Singular	my	mine
	your	yours
	his	his
	her	hers
Plural	our	ours
	your	yours
	their	theirs

B1 - B2

*Possessive pronouns are words used to identify persons or things that belong to the owner. Possessive pronouns are used without a noun, unlike **possessive adjectives** which always accompany a noun.*

B2. Possessive Pronouns

This cat is **mine**.

This dog is **yours**.

These birds are **his**.

This duck is **hers.**

Those chickens are **ours**.

Those hens are **yours**.

That bull is **theirs**.

B3. Possessive Adjectives and Pronouns

adj	I like **my** dog.
pro	The dog is **mine.**
adj	You like **your** horse.
pro	The horse is **yours.**
adj	He likes **his** cat.
pro	The cat is **his.**
adj	She likes **her** duck.
pro	The duck is **hers.**

B4. Possessive Adjectives and Pronouns

adj	We like **our** ox.
pro	The ox is **ours**.
adj	They like **their** cows.
pro	The cows are **theirs**.
adj	You like **your** calf.
pro	The calf is **yours**.
adj	Lucy likes **her** chickens.
pro	The chickens are **hers**.

B4 - B5

Possessive pronouns are words used to identify persons or things that belong to the owner. Possessive pronouns are used without a noun, unlike possessive adjectives which always accompany a noun.

B5. Possessive Pronouns: Questions

Is this coat yours?
Yes, it is mine.

Are those sweaters hers?
No, they are ours.

Are the blue shirts theirs?
Yes, they are theirs.

Is this desk his?
No, it is mine.

B6. Model Verb "can-could": Possibility

B6 (Review)

I cannot do it now.
I **could** do it tomorrow.

She can't come today.
She **could** come tomorrow.

They cannot accuse Mary.
They **could** accuse Tom.

We can't say yes now.
We **could** say yes tomorrow.

C1. Read and Listen to the story.

Sometimes my wife and I spend a few weeks with the family of my wife. It is a big family: three brothers, three sisters and two uncles. There are many animals on their family farm: ten cows, one ox, five horses and seven dogs.

The cows belong to **one** of the brothers. They are **his**. The ox belongs to the **uncles**. It is **theirs**. One horse belongs to **one** of the sisters. It is **hers**. The rest of the horses belong to the other **sisters**. They are **theirs**. The dogs are **ours**.

Besides these animals, there are many other animals walking or running around the farm: sheep, rabbits, hens and chickens.

C2. Read and Listen to the story.

Mrs. Gray prepares dinner every day. She usually cooks beef or turkey for dinner. There is plenty of beef and chicken in the freezer, but there is not much fish. The children don't care much for fish.

They start dinner with a bowl of soup. They like homemade soup, especially chicken soup. They hate canned soup. After eating the soup, Mrs. Gray serves the main course. This course consists of meat or fish with potatoes, rice or vegetables.

There is always some dessert after dinner. It consists of a piece of cake, a few cookies or a lot of ice cream.

D1. Tom / backyard

What does Tom have?
He has a deer.

Where is the deer?
It is in the backyard.

Is this his deer?
Yes, this deer is his.

D2. parents / kitchen

What do your parents have?
They have a cat.

Where is the cat?
It is in the kitchen.

Is this their cat?
Yes, this cat is theirs.

D3. Martha / backyard

What does Martha have?
She has a dog.

Where is the dog?
It is in the backyard.

Is this her dog?
Yes, this dog is hers.

D4. you / tree

What do you have?
I have some birds.

Where are the birds?
They are in the tree.

Are these your birds?
Yes, these birds are mine.

Feeling better

1. *How are you feeling?*
2. I feel much better.
3. My headache is gone.
4. My finger doesn't bother me anymore.
5. The wound is healed.
6. The infection is cured.
7. I don't feel pain in my tooth.
8. I am almost normal.
9. My cold is getting better.
10. It is nothing serious anymore.

For the English audio pronunciations and written native language translations of **section E,** please go to:

www.basicesl.com

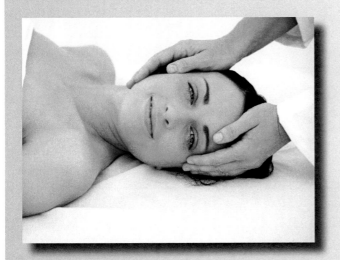

My headache is gone.

My finger doesn't bother me anymore.

End of the **oral exercises** for lesson 13.
You can find additional exercises in sections D, F & G at Basic ESL Online.

Please continue with the **written exercises** for this lesson in **section H**.

H1. Write the possessive adjective and pronoun corresponding to the owner.

Owner	Possessive Adjective	Possessive Pronoun
1. I	*my*	*mine*
2. You		
3. He		
4. She		
5. We		
6. They		
7. Sharon		
8. The school		
9. Paul		
10. The men		
11. Mary and I		
12. My family		
13. Carl and you		
14. Henry and Sheryl		
15. The students		
16. My house		

H2. Follow the example.

1. Jane rides **her** own horse.   *The horse is **hers**.*

2. I have **my** own dogs.   _____

3. We buy **our** own deer.   _____

4. Mike wears **his** own clothes.   _____

5. They prefer **their** own cats.   _____

6. You like **your** own house.   _____

7. Janet uses **her** own combs.   _____

H3. Answer with possessive pronouns.

1. Is this **your** shirt?   *No, this shirt is not **mine**.*

2. Is this **his** car?   _____

3. Are these **her** clothes?   _____

4. Is this **their** book?   _____

5. Is this **our** school?   _____

6. Are these **my** keys?   _____

7. Are these **your** dogs?   _____

H4. Complete with the corresponding possessive adjective or pronoun.

1. I don't have *my* watch and you don't have _____ .

2. Greg wears _____ shoes. I wear _____ .

3. Carol spends _____ money and we spend _____ .

4. We like _____ car. Carol likes _____ .

5. Carol drives _____ car. We drive _____ .

6. I clean _____ own plate. Do they clean _____ ?

7. No, they don't clean _____ own plates, but they clean _____ rooms.

H5. Change the statements to questions.

1. The dot is inside the circle.   *Is the dot inside the circle?*

2. Pat studied a lot yesterday.   _____

3. She always studies math.   _____

4. There are two dogs here.   _____

5. They can be bad.   _____

6. Ann was traveling.   _____

7. Ann does not travel alone.   _____

8. Ray didn't say that.   _____

9. Ray did not talk to Liz.   _____

10. Ray talked to you.   _____

11. Ray can't talk now.   _____

H6. Ask the questions corresponding to these answers.

1. **My mom** prepares dinner.   *Who prepares dinner?*

2. Her name is **Carol**.   _____

3. She's **55 years** old.   _____

4. She prepares dinner **at noon**.   _____

5. She usually cooks **turkey**.   _____

6. She buys turkey at **the store**.   _____

7. Turkey costs **$3.00** lb.   _____

8. She buys **2** turkeys.   _____

9. The turkeys are very **tasty**.   _____

10. They are **white**.   _____

11. Mary likes turkey **a lot**.   _____

H7. Rewrite the story. Change *every week* for *last week.*

Every week Carl **helps** his dad in the garden. His father **rewards** him with a twenty dollar bill. Carl **is** very happy. He **plans** to save enough money to buy a bicycle.

As soon as Carl **receives** the money from his father, he **walks** to the bank and **changes** the 20 dollar bill for a ten dollar bill, a five dollar bill and several coins.

Every week Carl **saves** the ten dollar bill for his bicycle. His cousin **borrows** the five dollar bill and **deposits** the bill in the bank. With the rest of the money Carl **invites** his friends to an ice-cream.

Last week _____

_____

_____

_____

_____

_____

_____

_____

_____

_____

_____

_____

_____

_____

_____

_____

_____

_____

Lesson #14

Wild Animals

Index

Audio & Translations

English Audio available online for sections A-E.

Translations in various Languages available online for Sections A, B, and E.

www.BasicESL.com

1. buffalo

2. boar

3. tiger

4. wolf

5. lion

6. crocodile

7. elephant

8. rhinoceros

9. hippopotamus

10. bear

11. leopard

12. bull

13. giraffe

14. snake

15. bison

16. panther

17. fox

18. coyote

19. gorilla

20. kangaroo

21. monkey

22. lizard

23. polar bear

24. skunk

Other Vocabulary

1.	n	group	**7.**	adj	dangerous	**13.**	v	encourage
2.	n	danger	**8.**	adj	horrible	**14.**	v	frighten
3.	n	tree	**9.**	v	awful	**15.**	v	hope
4.	adj	famous	**10.**	v	sign up	**16.**	v	join
5.	adj	careful	**11.**	v	stray	**17.**	v	talk
6.	adj	wild	**12.**	v	advise	**18.**	con	warn

B1. Comparison of Adjectives

ℹ	A	He is **tall**.
	C	He is **taller** than Ann.
	S	He is **the tallest** at school.
	A	You are **smart**.
	C	You are **smarter** than John.
	S	You are **the smartest** in the class.
	A	Ann is **happy**.
	C	She is **happier** than Sue.
	S	She is **the happiest** girl of all.

B1

Adjectives (A) express qualities that describe nouns. These qualities have different degrees. There are two degrees of comparisons: **comparative (C)** degree and **superlative (S)** degree. The **comparative** degree compares the qualities between **two** people or things. The **superlative** degree states who possesses the **highest degree** of quality among various persons or things.

B2. Superiority: Short Adjectives

ℹ

Tom is **poor**.
Joe is **poorer** than Tom.

You are **young**.
I am **younger** than you.

My son is **short**.
My cousin is **shorter** than my son.

The student is **tall**.
He is **taller** than the teacher.

B2 - B3

There are three kinds of **comparative forms** for adjectives: **superiority, inferiority and equality.**

The comparative form of **superiority** indicates that one person or thing has a higher degree of quality than another. This comparison form depends on the number of syllables of the adjective.

Short adjectives are those with one syllable or with two syllables ending in "-y." One syllable short adjectives form the comparison of superiority by adding "-er" to the adjective. **For short adjectives ending in "-y,"** replace the "-y" with "-i" and add "-er."

B3. Superiority: Short Adjectives **ending in "-y"**

ℹ

Lesson 4 is **easy**.
Lesson 5 is **easier** than lesson 4.

Your sweater is **dirty**.
It is **dirtier** than your robe.

Margaret is **pretty**.
Jane is **prettier** than Margaret.

Your sons are **happy**.
They are **happier** than mine.

B4. Superiority: Short Adjectives ending in consonant

Our house is **big**.
Your house is **bigger** than ours.

The books are **thin**.
The notebooks are **thinner**.

His aunt is **fat**.
His uncle is **fatter** than his aunt.

The water is **hot**.
The soup is **hotter** than the water.

B4

*For one syllable adjectives ending in a **consonant** preceded by a **single** vowel, **double** the consonant before adding "-er."*

B5. Superiority: Irregular Comparisons

The lunch was **bad**.
The breakfast was **worse**.

My dad is **good**.
My mother is **better** than my father.

Chicago is **far**.
New York is **farther** than Chicago.

Mary has **little** money.
I have **less** money than Mary.

B5

Some adjectives use different words to form the comparisons.

B6. Superiority: Long Adjectives

A gorilla is **jealous**.
It is **more jealous** than a wolf.

A tiger is **beautiful**.
It is **more beautiful** than a monkey.

Paul is **famous**.
He is **more famous** that Peter.

John is a **common** name.
It is **more common** than Andrew.

B6

***Long adjectives** are those with 3 or more syllables and those with 2 syllables not ending in "-y."*

*They form the comparison of superiority with the adverb **"more"** in front of the adjective.*

C1. Read and Listen to the story.

Every year most of the students **sign up** for a trip to the famous Yellowstone National Park. They **carry** their sleeping bags. Eight teachers **accompany** the students. The principal **stays** at school. Some parents **join** the group in order to help the teachers.

Before leaving for Yellowstone Park, one of the teachers **advises** the students to be careful with wild animals, especially with scorpions, bears, snakes and wolves. He also **talks** about the dangers of straying away from the group. Luckily there are no lions, tigers, elephants or bulls at the park.

C2. Read and Listen to the dialog.

Today most of the students **are signing** up for a trip to the famous Yellowstone National Park. All of them **are carrying** their sleeping bags. Eight teachers **are accompanying** the students. The principal **is staying** at school. Some parents **are joining** the group in order to help the teachers.

Before leaving for Yellowstone Park, one of the teachers **is advising** the students to be careful with wild animals, especially with scorpions, bears, snakes and wolves. He also **is talking** about the dangers of straying away from the group. Luckily there are no lions, tigers, elephants or bulls at the park.

D1. tall / giraffe

Are lions tall?
Yes, they are tall.

Are they taller than giraffes?
No, giraffes are taller.

Are you sure?
Yes, I am 100% sure.

D2. powerful / rhinoceros

Are bison powerful?
Yes, they are powerful.

Are they more powerful than rhinoceros?
No, rhinoceros are more powerful.

Are you sure?
Yes, I am 100% sure.

D3. big / elephant

Are boars big?
Yes, they are big.

Are they bigger that elephants?
No, elephants are bigger.

Are you sure?
Yes, I am 100% sure.

D4. fast / horse

Are bulls fast?
Yes, they are fast.

Are they faster than horses?
No, horses are faster.

Are you sure?
Yes, I am 100% sure.

Else

1. What else did you see?
2. Who else is coming?
3. Whom else did you speak with?
4. How else did she react?
5. Where else can she be?
6. Get me something else.
7. Do as I say or else.
8. There is nothing else better.
9. No one else knows this.
10. I treated Fred like anyone else.

For the English audio pronunciations and written native language translations of **section E,** please go to:

www.basicesl.com

No one else knows this.

There is nothing else better.

End of the **oral exercises** for lesson 14.
You can find additional exercises in sections D, F & G at Basic ESL Online.

Please continue with the **written exercises** for this lesson in **section H**.

Lesson
14

H1. Write the comparative *form of superiority* of these adjectives.

1.	strong	*stronger*	awful	_____
2.	close	_____	bad	_____
3.	big	_____	sure	_____
4.	easy	_____	free	_____
5.	fat	_____	pretty	_____
6.	heavy	_____	famous	_____
7.	slow	_____	clear	_____
8.	strong	_____	fierce	_____
9.	tall	_____	serious	_____
10.	thin	_____	horrible	_____
11.	young	_____	hungry	_____
12.	little	_____	jealous	_____
13.	free	_____	small	_____
14.	hungry	_____	few	_____
15.	happy	_____	high	_____
16.	far	_____	wild	_____
17.	short	_____	lucky	_____
18.	many	_____	scary	_____

H2. Make comparisons of *superiority*.

1. **Your** house is expensive. **(My)**

   *My house is **more expensive than** your house.*

2. The **wolf** is fast. **(leopard)**

   _____

3. **English** is difficult. **(Spanish)**

   _____

4. The **gorilla** is big. **(orangutan)**

   _____

5. **Mary** is beautiful. **(Cynthia)**

   _____

6. My **uncle** is good. **(aunt)**

   _____

7. **Our** grades in math are bad. **(Your)**

   _____

8. The **bulls** are fierce. **(tigers)**

   _____

9. Their **grandfather** was fat. **(grandmother)**

   _____

10. **Greg** has little money. **(Sharon)**

    _____

11. **Tampa** is famous. **(Las Vegas)**

    _____

12. **Chicago** is far from Los Angeles. **(New York)**

    _____

H3. Complete with quantity adjectives: *many, much, a lot of or lots of.*

1. I know **many** people in _____ places.

2. He buys _____ shirts. How _____ money does he spend?

3. How _____ paper do you need? I need _____ paper.

4. Ann does not need _____ apples. She needs _____ juice.

5. I don't eat _____ pie. _____ pies are not good.

6. My brothers eat _____ pie. I eat _____ pie, too.

7. Do you see _____ fruit at the fruit stand? No, I don't see _____ fruits.

8. I see _____ vegetables, but t I don't see _____ kinds of fruits.

9. There is _____milk. There is not _____ sugar.

10. How _____ kinds of sugar do you use? I do not use _____ sugar.

H4. Make comparisons using adjectives.

1. The tomatoes cost $5.00 lb. The potatoes cost $2.00 lb.
   The tomatoes are more expensive than the potatoes.

2. The bookcase is 36" wide. The door is 24" wide.
   _____

3. Jenifer is 6' tall. John is 5'4" tall.
   _____

4. Mr. Perez is 70 years old. Mr. Smith is 68 years old.
   _____

5. The white shirt is size 15. The black one is size 14.
   _____

6. My street is 2 miles long. Your street is 100 yards long.
   _____

7. My worse grade in math is 8. Your best grade in math is 6.
   _____

H5. Follow the example.

1.   tall / lion

     giraffe

Who is taller, the giraffe or the lion?
     The giraffe is taller than the lion.
     The lion is shorter than the giraffe.

2.   strong / buffalo

     elephant

_____
_____
_____

3.   heavy / boar

     bear

_____
_____
_____

4.   beautiful / bison

     tiger

_____
_____
_____

5.   big / lizard

     rat

_____
_____
_____

Lesson #15

Other Animals

Index

Audio & Translations

English Audio available online for sections A-E.

Translations in various Languages available online for Sections A, B, and E.

www.BasicESL.com

10. octopus

11. whale

12. penguin

13. crab

14. seal

15. pelican

16. dolphin

17. shark

18. ant

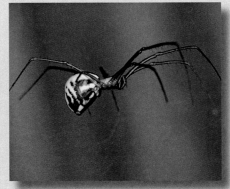

1. turtle

2. spider

3. bee

4. scorpion

5. fly

6. butterfly

7. eagle

8. cardinal

9. fish

19. flamingo

20. frog

21. lobster

22. owl

23. vulture

24. mosquito

Other Vocabulary

1.	n	bay	**7.**	adj	hollow	**13.**	v	hurt
2.	n	ocean	**8.**	adj	rare	**14.**	v	jump
3.	adj	ancient	**9.**	v	bite	**15.**	v	kill
4.	adj	brief	**10.**	v	fight	**16.**	v	scare
5.	adj	dull	**11.**	v	harm	**17.**	v	swallow
6.	adj	empty	**12.**	v	hit	**18.**	v	tear

B1. Adjectives: Comparison of Inferiority

Tom is strong.
Bill is **less** strong **than** Tom.
He is **not as** strong **as** Tom.

Mary is tall.
Lucy is **less** tall **than** Mary.
She is **not as** tall **as** Mary.

Paul is jealous.
Paul is **less** jealous **than** Rick.
He is **not as** jealous **as** Rick.

B2. Adjectives: Comparison of Inferiority

I am intelligent.
I am **less** intelligent **than** you.
I am **not as** intelligent **as** you.

The whale is big.
The shark is **less** big **than** the whale.
The shark is **not as** big **as** the whale.

The lake is deep.
The river is **less** deep **than** the lake.
The river is **not as** deep **as** the lake.

B3. Adjectives: Comparison of Equality

My uncle is old.
My aunt is **as** old **as** my uncle.

Jane is good.
Mark is **as** good **as** Jane.

A bear is aggressive.
A lion is **as** aggressive **as** the bear.

A hawk flies high.
A vulture flies **as** high **as** the hawk.

B1 - B2

The comparative form of inferiority is used to express an inferior degree of quality. It is formed with the adverb "less" or the words "not as" before the adjective.

B3

The comparative form of equality is used to compare nouns with the same degree of quality. It is formed with the word "as" before and after the adjective.

B4. Adjectives: Comparison of Equality

The school is far.
The hospital is **as** far **as** the school.

The cat is hungry.
The dog is **as** hungry **as** the cat.

The spider is tiny.
The fly is **as** tiny **as** the spider.

The pig is fat.
This dog is **as** fat **as** a pig.

B4

The **comparative form of equality** is used to compare nouns with the **same** degree of quality. It is formed with the word **"as"** before and after the adjective.

B5. Information Question Words

Information desired	Question words used
People	*Who is cooking?*
Things	*What is Mark cooking?*
Distance	*How far is the train station?*
Direction	*Which way is the airport?*
Number	*How many tickets do you want?*
Quantity	*How much money do you have?*

B6. Information Question Words

Information desired	Question words used
Manner	*How do you feel?*
Selection	*Which book do you prefer?*
Name	*What is her name?*
Age	*How old is she?*
Location	*Where does she live?*
Description	*What is she like?*

C1. Read and Listen to the story.

Last year most of the students **signed up** for an ocean trip. It started in San Francisco Bay. Eight teachers **accompanied** the students. Some parents **joined** the group in order to help the teachers.

Before leaving, one of the teachers **advised** them to be careful with whales, sharks, seals and dolphins. She also **talked** about other sea animals such as turtles, octopus, crabs, pelicans and seagulls.

After the trip, the teachers **invited** the students to eat lobster. It **was** a wonderful trip. They plan to sign up for the same trip next year.

C2. Read and Listen to the dialog.

Where are the students going?
They are going on a trip.

Where is the trip starting?
It is starting in San Francisco.

What kind of a trip?
A trip on the ocean.

How far do they sail?
They sail pretty far.

How many signed up for the trip?
Most of the students did.

Do they know how to swim?
Yes, they do.

Who joined the group?
Some parents joined the group.

Do they watch many sharks?
They generally don't.

Are there any teachers going too?
Only eight teachers are going.

What animals do they see?
They see whales and dolphins.

D1. colorful / spider

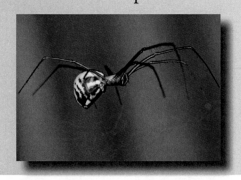

Is the spider colorful?
Yes, it is colorful.

Is it as colorful as the butterfly?
No, it is not as colorful.

Butterflies are more colorful.
Spiders are less colorful

D2. powerful / penguin

Is the penguin powerful?
Yes, it is powerful.

Is it as powerful as the seal?
No, it is not as powerful.

Seals are more powerful.
Penguins are less powerful.

D3. aggressive / whale

Is the whale aggressive?
Yes, it is aggressive.

Is it as aggressive as the shark?
No, it is not as aggressive.

Sharks are more aggressive.
Whales are less aggressive.

D4. expensive / crab

Is the crab expensive?
Yes, it is expensive.

Is it as expensive as the lobster?
No, it is not as expensive.

Lobsters are more expensive.
Crabs are less expensive.

Using the phone

1. The phone is ringing.
2. Pick up the phone.
3. Wait for the tone.
4. Dial the number.
5. The line is busy.
6. I dialed the wrong number.
7. Hang up the phone.
8. The phone does not work.
9. I got disconnected.

For the English audio pronunciations and written native language translations of **section E,** please go to:

www.basicesl.com

The phone is ringing.

The phone is dead.

End of the **oral exercises** for lesson 15.
You can find additional exercises in sections D, F & G at Basic ESL Online.

Please continue with the **written exercises** for this lesson in **section H**.

H - Written Exercises

15-10

Lesson **15**

H1. Make comparisons of equality.

1. **small**	This frog is	*as small as*	that lizard.
2. **tall**	A vulture is	_____	an eagle.
3. **generous**	My uncle is	_____	my aunt.
4. **clean**	Room 14 is	_____	room 15.
5. **beautiful**	My nieces are	_____	my sisters.
6. **bad**	Foxes are	_____	coyotes.
7. **good**	The pears are	_____	the apples.

H2. Make comparisons of inferiority.

1. **dangerous**	Snakes are	*less* dangerous **than**	bears.
	Snakes are	*not as* dangerous **as**	bears.
2. **heavy**	Boars are	_____	pigs.
	Boars are	_____	pigs.
3. **tall**	Buffaloes are	_____	giraffes.
	Buffaloes are	_____	giraffes.
4. **wild**	Bison are	_____	elephants.
	Bison are	_____	elephants.

H3. Make comparisons.

1. **amusing** The penguin is *as amusing* **as** the frog.
2. **happy** Sara is _____ **than** Caroline.
3. **handsome** Tom is _____ **than** Henry.
4. **heavy** The box is _____ **than** the sack.
5. **good** My nieces are _____ **than** my sisters.
6. **good** Fish is _____ **as** meat.
7. **bad** Supper was _____ **than** dinner.
8. **bad** This peach is _____ **as** that melon.
9. **tasty** Cherries are _____ **than** plums.
10. **aggressive** The shark is _____ **than** the whale.
11. **cheap** Cookies are _____ **than** chocolate.
12. **young** My brother is _____ **than** Mike.
13. **poisonous** The scorpion is _____ **as** the snake.
14. **thin** The notebook is _____ **than** the book.
15. **easy** Lesson 10 is _____ **than** lesson 20.
16. **easy** Lesson 4 is _____ **as** lesson 3.
17. **happy** Mary is _____ **than** Rudy.
18. **tall** The girl is _____ **than** the boy.
19. **hungry** I am _____ **as** you are.
20. **hungry** The poor are _____ **than** we are.
21. **polite** Jennifer is _____ **as** you.
22. **fast** A leopard runs _____ **than** a bear.
23. **fast** A tiger is _____ **as** a lion.
24. **long** The table is _____ **than** the desk.

H4. Circle the correct answer.

1. **An animal that hops.**	octopus	frog	crab	dolphin
2. **An animal with wings.**	boar	turtle	whale	bee
3. **An animal with a hump.**	mule	crocodile	camel	bat
4. **An animal with a long tail.**	penguin	goat	rat	tiger
5. **The tallest animal of all.**	elephant	lion	zebra	giraffe
6. **A scary animal.**	swan	cockroach	sheep	butterfly
7. **Who spins a web?**	butterfly	owl	spider	eagle

H5. Multiple choice. Choose the correct answer.

1. A lizard is not _____ dangerous as a spider.   **as**, more, than
2. A zebra is bigger _____ a monkey.   less, more, than
3. A hen is _____ slow than a rabbit.   less, more, than
4. A deer is _____ beautiful than a goat.   as, less, more
5. Oxen are slower _____ horses.   less, more, than
6. Cats are as nice _____ dogs.   as, less, than
7. Meat is _____ expensive as fish.   as, tasty, more
8. Cindy is _____ than Sue.   more pretty, prettier
9. Fred is_____ than Mike.   better, more good
10. English is _____ as Spanish.   as easy, easier, more easy
11. Lobster tastes _____ than crab.   cheaper, worse, as good
12. The name "Peter" is _____ than Hansel.   common, more common
13. This dog is _____ than the cat.   as nice, nicer, more nice

H6. Rewrite the story. Change *every year* for *last year.*

Every year most of the students **sign up** for a trip to Yellowstone National Park. They **carry** their sleeping bags.

Eight popular teachers **accompany** the students. The principal **stays** at school. Some parents **join** the group in order to help the teachers.

Before leaving for Yellowstone Park, one of the teachers **advises** the students to be careful with the wild animals. Especially he **mentions** scorpions, bears, snakes and wolves.

He also **talks** about the dangers of straying away from the group. He does not **mean** to frighten the students. Luckily **there are** no lions, and tigers at the park.

Last year _____

_____

_____

_____

_____

_____

_____

_____

_____

_____

_____

_____

_____

_____

_____

_____

_____

_____

_____

_____

ANSWER KEY SECTION

BASIC ESL WORKBOOK LEVEL 2

H1

1. There is
2. There are
3. There is
4. There are
5. There is
6. There are
7. There is
8. There are
9. There are
10. There is
11. There are
12. There is
13. There is

H2

1. Is there any chocolate?
2. Are there any peaches?
3. Is there any bacon today?
4. Are there any fried eggs?
5. Is there soup for lunch?
6. Are there some apples?
7. Is there salad today?
8. Is there some coffee?
9. Are there sausages for lunch?
10. Are there all kinds of tea?

H3

1. Yes, there is some.
   No, there isn't any.
2. Yes, there are some.
   No, there aren't any.
3. Yes, there are some.
   No, there aren't any.
4. Yes, there is some.
   No, there isn't any.
5. Yes, there are some.
   No, there aren't any.

H4

1. There is no chocolate.
   There isn't any chocolate.
2. There are no peaches.
   There aren't any peaches.
3. There is no bacon today.
   There isn't any bacon today.
4. There are no fried eggs.
   There aren't any fried eggs.
5. There is no soup for lunch.
   There isn't any soup for lunch.
6. There are no apples today.
   There aren't any apples today.
7. There is no salad today.
   There isn't any salad today.
8. There is no coffee.
   There isn't any coffee.
9. There are no sausages for lunch.
   There aren't any sausages for...

H5

1.
Is there any fruit for breakfast?
Yes, there is some fruit for breakfast.
Is there any fruit for lunch?
No, there is no fruit for lunch.

2.
Are there any sweets for breakfast?
No, there are no sweets for breakfast.
Are there any sweets for lunch?
Yes, there are some sweets for lunch.

3.
Is there any fish for breakfast?
Yes, there is some fish for breakfast.
Is there any fish for lunch?
No, there is no fish for lunch.

4.
Is there any soup for breakfast?
No, there is no soup for breakfast.
Is there any soup for lunch?
Yes, there is some soup for lunch.

5.
Are there any pies for breakfast?
Yes, there are some pies for breakfast.
Are there any pies for lunch?
No, there are no pies for lunch.

H1

	C	NC
1. bed	X	
2. bottle	X	
3. bowl	X	
4. biscuits	X	
5. butter		X
6. cake	X	
7. can	X	
8. loaf	X	
9. meat		X
10. pantry	X	
11. pie	X	
12. pillow	X	
13. sugar		X
14. salt		X

H2

1. How many
2. How many
3. How much
4. How much
5. How many
6. How much
7. How much
8. How many

H3

	A few	Lots of	Many
1. I have	X	X	X
I don't have			X
2. I eat	X	X	X
I don't eat			X
3. She needs	X	X	X
She does not need			X
4. Tom buys	X	X	X
Tom doesn't buy			X
5. They order	X	X	X
They don't order			X

H4

	a little	a lot	much
1. I have	X	X	
I don't have			X
2. I eat	X	X	
I don't eat			X
3. She needs	X	X	
She does not need			X
4. Tom buys	X	X	
Tom doesn't buy			X
5. They order	X	X	
They don't order			X

H5

1. many
2. a lot of
3. many
4. many, lots of
5. a lot of, a little
6. much
7. many
8. many, lots of
9. much
10. a lot of, a little
11. lot of
12. many
13. a lot of, a little
14. much
15. many, lots of
16. many

H6

1. I have a lot of fruit.
I don't have many vegetables.
I like fruit a lot.
I don't like vegetables much.

2. Ryan has many sweets.
He doesn't have much cheese.
He likes sweets a lot.
He doesn't like cheese much.

3. We have a lot of ice-cream.
We don't have many cookies.
We like ice-cream a lot.
We don't like cookies much.

4. My parents have many bottles of wine.
They don't have much coffee.
They like wine a lot.
They don't like coffee much.

5. You have a lot of honey.
You don't have many eggs.
You like honey a lot.
You don't like eggs much.

H1

1. pours
2. cries
3. stirs
4. studies
5. carries
6. multiplies
7. fixes
8. catches
9. tries
10. finishes
11. watches
12. brushes
13. needs
14. flies

H2

1. Tom blends the juices.
2. Tom enjoys the wine.
3. Tom mixes the fruits.
4. Tom bakes the pies.
5. Tom fries the chicken.
6. Tom plays at school.
7. Tom does homework.

H3

1. He does not use much...
2. He doesn't drink much...
3. They don't eat much...
4. There is not much...
5. We don't buy many...
6. She doesn't need many...
7. I don't want much...
8. He doesn't cut many...
9. She doesn't bake many...
10. Sara doesn't wash many...

H4

1. They like the meat sausages.
2. There are no fruit juices.
3. Where are the pies?
4. Those are big potatoes.
5. Where do they keep the forks?
6. We like the strawberry cakes.
7. You don't like soups.
8. They pour the wines.
9. The men wrap the sandwiches.
10. The women melt the cheese.

H5

Every day **my mom prepares** the main meal. **She starts** with the soup. **She makes** their favorite pea soup. **She washes** the peas in a saucepan, **drains** the water and **adds** clean water. Then **she boils** the soup on the stove.

While the soup is boiling, **she prepares** the main course of meat with onions. **She trims** the fat from the meat and **sprinkles** the meat with a little salt. **She chops** an onion and **fries** the meat with onion.

For dessert **she prepares** a fruit salad. **She splits** a melon and **removes** the seeds. Then **she peels** an orange and **mixes** the orange with the melon.

H6

1. jam
2. cabbage
3. Fish
4. milk
5. spaghetti
6. butter

H7

1. a lot of
2. much
3. much
4. many, lots of
5. many
6. eat
7. eats
8. eating
9. studying
10. study

H1

1. was
2. were
3. were
4. was
5. were
6. was
7. were

H2

1. They were not very far.
2. It was not low.
3. He was not in the last row.
4. The river was not close.
5. It was not an even number.
6. She was not living here.
7. They were not poor.

H3

1. one, ten
2. two, twenty
3. three, thirty
4. four, forty
5. five, fifty
6. six, sixty
7. seven, seventy
8. eight, eighty
9. nine, ninety
10. zero, one hundred

H4

1. weren't
2. wasn't
3. wasn't
4. weren't
5. wasn't
6. wasn't
7. weren't
8. wasn't

H5

1. 52, 16, 18
2. 7, 11, 25
3. 55
4. =
5. New York
6. northern

H6

1. Was Tony working?
2. Were we watching TV?
3. Does he know the distance?
4. Was the palace far away?
5. Does she have three rulers?
6. Was there a lot of traffic?
7. Do they underline the words?
8. Were they two miles away?
9. Was it not far?
10. Do you realize that?
11. Does he climb the hill?

H7

1. Where were you yesterday?
I was in downtown.
How far is downtown from the river?
It is seventy miles away.

2. Where was Jane yesterday?
She was on the mountain.
How far is the mountain from the freeway?
It is forty miles away.

3. Where were the children yesterday?
They were at school.
How far is the school from the park?
It is ninety yards away.

4. Where was John yesterday?
He was at the palace.
How far is the palace from the lake?
It is fifty miles away.

K - Lesson 5 - Level II — Chapter 2

H1

1. west
2. north
3. southern
4. eastern
5. few
6. few
7. left
8. far
9. far
10. last
11. less
12. previous

H2

1. I was going...
2. I wasn't going...
3. You were studying...
4. You weren't playing...
5. Greg was going...
6. He wasn't going...

H3

1. The children are sleeping.
2. The men were far away.
3. The women prepare the meals.
4. They prefer gray skirts.
5. We weren't at home.
6. These are your last grades.
7. Those are big potatoes.
8. The girls are nice.
9. They like the sausages.
10. The children are sleeping.
11. They clean the dirty dishes.

H4

1. many
2. much, a lot
3. many, few
4. lots of, many
5. a little, a few
6. many, a lot of
7. a lot, much
8. a lot of, many
9. much, a lot
10. much, a few

H5

1. Where is Boston?
It is in the east.
Is Boston an eastern city?
Yes, it is.
How far from Boston do you live?
I live fifty miles away.

2. Where is San Francisco?
It is in the west.
Is San Francisco a western city?
Yes, it is.
How far from San Francisco does Liz live?
She lives sixty miles away.

3. Where is Houston?
It is in the south.
Is Houston a southern city?
Yes, it is.
How far from Houston do the parents live?
They live forty miles away.

4. Where is Chicago?
It is in the north.
Is Chicago a northern city?
Yes, it is.
How far from Chicago does the sister live?
She lives eighty miles away.

H6

Janet is making plans to visit southern California. She begins her trip in Los Angeles. She is taking freeway 5 to San Francisco.

Janet prefers this route because she has a friend in Fresno. From there she continues her trip to San Francisco.

She passes through Sacramento, the capital of the state. She plans to visit this city on her way back to Los Angeles.

H7

1. She wants to see southern California.
2. The trip starts in Los Angeles.
3. She is planning to go to San Francisco.
4. Because she has a friend in Fresno.
5. No, she is planning to visit Sacramento on her way back from San Francisco.

H1

1. Do not open the book.
2. Let us not close the books.
3. Let us not start the test.
4. Do not get on the bus.
5. Let us not take a seat.
6. Do not take a seat.
7. Let us not stand up.
8. Do not ring the bell.

H2

1. Don't turn left.
2. Let's not sit down.
3. Don't get on the bus.
4. Let's not walk.
5. Don't take a seat.
6. Let's not wait for the bus.
7. Don't take bus no. 40.

H3

1. Wait for the bus.
   Don't wait for the train.
2. Ho to school.
   Don't go home.
3. Take off your shirt.
   Don't take off your T-shirt.
4. Get on bus 40.
   Don't get on bus 50.
5. Write with pen.
   Don't write with pencil.
6. Turn left.
   Don't turn right.

H4

1. Fifty-five minus twenty-two is thirty-three.
2. Forty-four times two is eighty-eight.
3. Sixty-six plus eleven is seventy-seven.

H5

1. What was your uncle like?
2. How much meat does Ann eat?
3. Who is thin?
4. How far was the church?
5. What was beautiful?
6. Which way does Ann go to church?
7. Where is Mary?
8. What is she eating?
9. What does her sister like?
10. How many sandwiches does Tony eat?
11. What color is his shirt?
12. What is brown?
13. How far away was Sara?
14. How many miles away was Tony?
15. How many lamps does Henry have?
16. How much sugar does Mary use?
17. Who is wrong?
18. How old is he?
19. Where is Mary traveling?
20. How far is it?
21. How much is two plus two?
22. What is Mary like?
23. Which way was she going?
24. How fast was she driving?

H6

When you leave the bus station, turn left.
Walk to the corner of 12th Street and K Ave.
Turn left and walk two blocks.
Cross 10th street.
Turn left and cross K Avenue.
Walk half a block to the bus stop.
Take bus 25.
Get off at the next bus stop.
Ho back to the corner of M Avenue.
Turn left and walk half a block.
The entrance is on your left side.

H7

1. is
2. was
3. were
4. are
5. far
6. way
7. many
8. Who
9. through
10. from

H1

1.	blessed	achieved
2.	carried	calculated
3.	closed	chopped
4.	collected	copied
5.	compared	faded
6.	delayed	gained
7.	filled	lifted
8.	fried	planned
9.	mixed	promised
10.	opened	cried
11.	pulled	stayed
12.	studied	stirred
13.	trimmed	stopped
14.	walked	waited
15.	worried	washed
16.	crossed	changed

H2

1. He opened...
2. We waited...
3. The bus stopped...
4. Mary washed...
5. I visited...
6. Mom trimmed...
7. Sara studied...
8. The child cried...
9. They asked...
10. They copied...
11. He filled...
12. Susan fried...
13. They stayed...
14. They cried...
15. Mom chopped...
16. I worried...
17. Carol washed...
18. This fabric was
19. We studied...
20. The man blessed...
21. I planned...
22. Dad trimmed...
23. My aunt stirred...
24. She mixed...

H3

1. How long is the table?
   What is the length of the table?
2. How wide is the desk?
   What is the width of the desk?
3. How tall is Henry?
   What is the height of Henry?
4. How deep is the river?
   What is the depth of the river?
5. How high is the building?
   What is the height of the building?
6. How old is Diane?
   What is the age of Diane?
7. How long is the ruler?
   What is the length of the ruler?
8. How big is the table?
   What is the size of the table?

H4

Last year Mrs. Gray **prepared** the dinners. She usually **cooked** meat or turkey for dinner. There **was** plenty of meat or chicken in the freezer, but there **were** not many vegetables.

The big family **started** dinner with a bowl of soup. The children **liked** homemade soup mainly, especially chicken soup. They **hated** canned soup.

After eating the soup, Mrs. Gray **served** the main course. It **consisted** of meat with potatoes, rice or green vegetables.

There **were** always some desserts for dinner. Their favorite one **was** ice-cream.

H1

1. She did not peel...
2. I did not remove...
3. You did not lift...
4. Tom did not trim...
5. We did not love...
6. They did not call...
7. I did not chop...
8. He did not walk...
9. He did not stop...
10. They did not wash...
11. They did not cry...
12. We did not copy...
13. They did not bless...
14. He did not travel...
15. They did not wrap...
16. They did not delay...

H2

1. pound
2. ounce
3. dozen
4. gallon
5. quarts
6. one foot
7. two feet
8. one inch
9. two inches
10. kilometer

H3

100	one hundred
200	two hundred
300	three hundred
400	four hundred
500	five hundred
600	six hundred
700	seven hundred
800	eight hundred
900	nine hundred
120	one hundred and twenty

H4

1. don't
2. isn't
3. didn't
4. doesn't
5. aren't
6. don't
7. weren't
8. doesn't
9. isn't
10. didn't
11. wasn't
12. aren't

H5

1. **How much does the meat cost?**
   It costs five dollars a pound.
   Please, give half a pound of meat.
2. **How much does the juice cost?**
   It costs two dollars a gallon.
   Please, give me half a gallon of juice.
3. **How much do the eggs cost?**
   They cost three dollars a dozen.
   Please, give me half a dozen eggs.
4. **How much does the perfume cost?**
   It costs nine dollars an ounce.
   Please, give me half an ounce of ...
5. **How much do the melons cost?**
   They cost four dollars each.
   Please, give me half a melon...

H6

1. D
2. D
3. D
4. D
5. Ed
6. Ed
7. T
8. D
9. Ed
10. D
11. Ed
12. D
13. T
14. T

H7

Last year Henry **walked** to the lake. Some of his friends **accompanied** Henry to the lake. His parents **stayed** at home.

Henry **preferred** to buy five pounds of meat. His friends **wanted** to bring some fish. All **agreed** on the salad and the drinks.

When they **arrived** at the lake, they **rested** on the grass. Later they **crossed** the lake in a boat and **started** fishing.

There **was** plenty of fish for everybody. Some of the fish **weighed** five pounds. Others **weighed** half a pound or few ounces. Henry **cooked** the fish. It **tasted** very good.

H1

1. **Did he carry...**
   Yes, he carried...
   No, he did not carry...
2. **Did she endorse...**
   Yes, she endorsed...
   No, she did not endorse...
3. **Did Ann copy...**
   Yes, she copied...
   No, she did not copy...
4. **Did she stop...**
   Yes, she stopped...
   No, she did not stop...
5. **Did she fry...**
   Yes, she fried...
   No, she did not fry...

H2

1. He buys thirty-three pounds of sugar.
2. They wanted twenty-two gallons of juice.
3. It purchased forty-four dozens of eggs.
4. It costs fifty-five cents an ounce.
5. They received sixty-six gold coins each.
6. He gained seventy-seven kilograms.

H3

1. Yes, I wanted ..
   No, I didn't want...
2. Yes, they agreed...
   No, they didn't agree...
3. Yes, she invited...
   No, she didn't invite...
4. Yes, he recognizes....
   No he doesn't recognize...
5. Yes, I attempted ...
   No, I didn't attempt...

H4

1. Yes, they are...
2. Yes, she learns...
3. Yes, she learned...
4. Yes, she studies...
5. Yes, she studied...
6. Yes, he purchased...
7. Yes, he likes...
8. Yes, they were...
9. Yes, she uses...
10. Yes, she wanted...
11. Yes, she wants...
12. Yes, she needs...
13. Yes, I needed...
14. Yes, he was looking...
15. Yes, it was...
16. Yes, I have...
17. Yes, I used...
18. Yes, he played...
19. Yes, he plays...
20. Yes, she complained...
21. Yes, she complains...
22. Yes, she is complaining...
23. Yes, I liked...
24. Yes, she enjoys...
25. Yes, she listened...
26. Yes, I am living...

H5

1. How much is a penny worth?
   It is worth one cent.
   How many pennies are there in one dollar?
   There are one hundred pennies in a dollar.

2. How much is a nickel worth?
   It is worth five cents.
   How many nickels are there in one dollar?
   There are twenty nickels in a dollar.

3. How much is a dime worth?
   It is worth ten cents.
   How many dimes are there in one dollar?
   There are ten dimes in a dollar.

4. How much is a quarter worth?
   It is worth twenty-five cents.
   How many quarters are there in one dollar?
   There are four quarters in a dollar.

H1

1.	I cannot...	I can't...
2.	He cannot...	He can't...
3.	We cannot...	We can't...
4.	You cannot...	You can't...
5.	She cannot...	She can't...
6.	They cannot...	They can't...
7.	Sara cannot...	Sara can't...

H2

1.	They could not	They couldn't
2.	He could not	He couldn't
3.	We could not	We couldn't
4.	You could not	You couldn't
5.	She could not	She couldn't
6.	They could not	They couldn't
7.	Sara could not	Sara couldn't

H5

1.	in	11.	at
2.	at	12.	on
3.	in	13.	in
4.	to	14.	on
5.	in	15.	in
6.	to	16.	on
7.	on	17.	in
8.	to	18.	to
9.	at	19.	in
10.	on	20.	on

H6

1. Don't stay behind...
2. Don't go up...
3. Don't turn left.
4. Don't put...on ...
5. Don't write below...
6. Don't stay inside...
7. Don't put...on top of...
8. Don't keep... close to...
9. Don't sit close to...
10. Don't keep...out of ...

H3

1. Could they...
2. Can he...
3. Can we...
4. Can you...
5. Could he...
6. Can they...
7. Could Sara...
8. Can Mike...
9. Could Fred...
10. Can we....

H4

1. Yes, she can...
   No, she cannot...   No, she can't.
2. Yes, they can...
   No, they cannot..   No, they can't.
3. Yes, he can...
   No, he cannot...   No, he can't.
4. Yes, you can...
   No, you cannot...   No, you can't.
5. Yes, they can...
   No, they cannot..   No, they can't.

H7

1. What do you see in this picture?
   I see a dot and a circle.
   Where is the dot?
   It is on top of the circle.
   Where is the circle?
   It is under the dot.

2. What do you see in this picture?
   I see a dot and a circle.
   Where is the dot?
   It is inside the circle.
   Where is the circle?
   It is around the dot.

3. What do you see in this picture?
   I see a little girl and a desk.
   Where is the little girl?
   She is under the desk.
   Where is the desk?
   It is over the little girl.

4. What do you see in this picture?
   I see a thread and a girl.
   Where is the thread?
   It is through the needle.
   Where is the girl?
   She is against the wall.

H1

1.	One	1st	First
2.	Two	2nd	Second
3.	Three	3rd	Third
4.	Four	4th	Fourth
5.	Five	5th	Fifth
6.	Six	6th	Sixth
7.	Seven	7th	Seventh
8.	Eight	8th	Eighth
9.	Nine	9th	Ninth
10.	Ten	10th	Tenth

H2

1. Florida
2. Texas
3. California
4. Colorado
5. Arizona
6. New Mexico
7. New York
8. Wisconsin
9. Illinois
10. Alabama
11. Washington
12. Oregon

H3

1.	Yes, they did.	No, they didn't.
2.	Yes, I did.	No, I didn't.
3.	Yes, she did.	No, she didn't.
4.	Yes, she did.	No, she didn't.
5.	Yes, it did.	No, it didn't.
6.	Yes, they did.	No, we didn't.
7.	Yes, I did.	No, it didn't.

H4

1.	Yes, he does.	No, he doesn't.
2.	Yes, there are.	No, there aren't.
3.	Yes, I do.	No, I don't.
4.	Yes, I was.	No, I wasn't.
5.	Yes, it does.	No, it doesn't.
6.	Yes, there is.	No, there isn't.
7.	Yes, she was.	No, she wasn't.

H5

1. Were you there yesterday?
2. Did they cross the street...?
3. Is he working today?
4. Do you always study for the test?
5. What do you see in this picture?
6. Does Mary answer all the...
7. Did Mrs. Smith peel the...?

H6

1.
What do you see in the fifth picture?
I see several dots.
How many dots do you see?
I see five dots in the fifth picture.
Where is the green dot?
It is in the center.

2.
What do you see in the sixth picture?
I see several stars.
How many stars do you see?
I see six stars in the 6th picture.
Where is the red star?
It is in the upper right hand corner.

3.
What do you see in the seventh picture?
I see several pencils.
How many pencils do you see?
I see seven pencils in the seventh picture.
How long are the pencils?
They are nine inches long.

4.
What do you see in the eighth...
I see several envelopes.
How many envelopes do you see?
I see eight envelopes in the eight...
How much are the envelopes?
They are twenty-five cents each.

H7

Where did you use to live?
I used to live in Tampa, Florida.
My address was three hundred forty five Third Avenue.

Where did Paul use to live?
He used to live in Chicago, Illinois.
His address was eight hundred and six Eleventh Street.

Where did your parents use...?
They used to live in Dallas, Texas.
Their address was two hundred and twenty-seven Fourth Avenue.

Where did Liz use to live?
She used to live in Salem, Oregon.
Her address was five hundred eighty-nine Sixth Avenue.

H1

1.	slowly	7.	fully
2.	strongly	8.	easily
3.	bravely	9.	well
4.	carefully	10.	happily
5.	badly	11.	fast
6.	politely	12.	probably

H2

	Adj.	Adv.
1.	X	
2.		X
3.	X	
4.	X	
5.	X	
6.		X
7.	X	
8.		X

H3

1.	bad	badly
2.	easy	easily
3.	happy	happily
4.	slow	slowly
5.	strongly	strong
6.	quickly	quick
7.	good	well
8.	careful	carefully

H4

1. The table is big and old.
2. Yes, there is. There is a chair behind the table.
3. There are two pictures on the wall.
4. The big picture is 20" wide and 5' long.
5. No, he nails the pictures to the wall.
6. He keeps the small family pictures in the middle shelf.

H5

1. one
2. home
3. box
4. sixth
5. who
6. well

H6

1. in
2. at
3. of
4. on
5. for
6. Did
7. easily
8. easy
9. well
10. like

H1

1. my   mine
2. your   yours
3. his   his
4. her   hers
5. our   ours
6. their   theirs
7. her   hers
8. its
9. his   his
10. their   theirs
11. our   ours
12. its
13. your   yours
14. their   theirs
15. their   theirs
16. its

H2

1. The horse is hers.
2. The dogs are mine.
3. The deer is ours.
4. The clothes are his.
5. The cats are theirs.
6. The house is his(hers).
7. The combs are hers.

H3

1. No, this shirt is not mine.
2. No, this car is not his.
3. No, these clothes are not hers.
4. No, this book is not theirs.
5. No, this school is not ours.
6. No, theses keys are not yours.
7. No, these dogs are not mine.

H4

1. my   yours
2. his   mine
3. her   ours
4. our   hers
5. her   ours
6. my   theirs
7. their   their

H5

1. Is the box inside the circle?
2. Did Pat study a lot yesterday?
3. Does she always study math?
4. Are there two dogs here?
5. Can they be bad?
6. Was Ann traveling?
7. Doesn't Ann travel alone?
8. Didn't Ray say that?
9. Didn't Ray talk to Liz?
10. Did Ray talk to you?
11. Can't Ray talk now?

H6

1. Who prepares dinner?
2. What is her name?
3. How old is she?
4. When does she prepare dinner?
5. What does she usually cook?
6. Where does she buy turkey?
7. How much does the turkey cost?
8. How many turkeys does she buy?
9. How are the turkeys?
10. What color are they?
11. How much does Mary like turkey?

H7

Last week Carl **helped** his dad in the garden. His father **rewarded** him with a twenty dollar bill. Carl **is** very happy. He **plans** to save enough money to buy a bicycle.

As soon as Carl **received** the money from his father, he **walked** to the bank and **changed** the 20 dollar bill for a ten dollar bill, a five dollar bill and several coins.

Every week Carl **saved** the ten dollar bill for his bicycle. His cousin **borrowed** the five dollar bill and **deposited** the bill in the bank. With the rest of the money Carl **invited** his friends to an ice-cream.

H1

1.	stronger	more awful
2.	closer	worse
3.	bigger	more sure
4.	easier	more free
5.	fatter	prettier
6.	heavier	more famous
7.	slower	clearer
8.	stronger	more fierce
9.	taller	more serious
10.	thinner	more horrible
11.	younger	hungrier
12.	less	more jealous
13.	more free	smaller
14.	hungrier	fewer
15.	happier	higher
16.	farther	wilder
17.	shorter	luckier
18.	more	more scary

H2

1. My house is more expensive than yours.
2. The leopard is faster than the wolf.
3. Spanish is more difficult than English.
4. The orangutan is bigger than the gorilla.
5. Cynthia is more beautiful than Mary.
6. My aunt is better than my uncle.
7. Your grades in math are worse than ours.
8. The tigers are more fierce than the bulls.
9. The grandmother was fatter than...
10. Sharon has less money than Greg.
11. Las Vegas is more famous than Tampa.
12. New York is farther than Chicago.

H3

1.	many	many
2.	lots of	much
3.	much	a lot of
4.	many	a lot of
5.	much	Many
6.	a lot of	a lot of
7.	a lot of	many
8.	many	many
9.	a lot of	much
10.	many	much

H4

1. The tomatoes are more expensive than the potatoes.
2. The bookcase is wider than the door.
3. Jenifer is taller than John.
4. Mr. Perez is older than Mr. Smith.
5. The white shirt is bigger than the black one.
6. My street is longer than your street.
7. My grade in math is better than your grade in math.

H5

1. Who is taller, the giraffe or the lion?
The giraffe is taller than the lion.
The lion is shorter than the giraffe

2. Who is stronger, the elephant or the buffalo?
The elephant is stronger than the buffalo.
The buffalo is weaker than the elephant.

3. Who is heavier, the boar or the bear?
The bear is heavier than the boar.
The boar is lighter than the bear.

4. Who is more beautiful, the bison or the tiger?
The tiger is more beautiful than the bison.
The bison is uglier than the tiger.

5. Who is bigger, the lizard or the rat?
The rat is bigger than the lizard.
The lizard is smaller than the rat.

H1

1. as small as
2. as tall as
3. as generous as
4. as clean as
5. as beautiful as
6. as bad as
7. as good as

H2

1. less dangerous than
   not as dangerous as
2. less heavier than
   not as heavy as
3. less tall than
   not as tall as
4. less wild than
   not as wild as

H3

1. as amusing
2. happier
3. more handsome
4. heavier
5. better
6. as good
7. worse
8. as bad
9. tastier
10. more aggressive
11. cheaper
12. younger
13. as poisonous
14. thinner
15. easier
16. as easy
17. happier
18. taller
19. as hungry
20. hungrier
21. as polite
22. faster
23. as fast
24. longer

H4

1. frog
2. bee
3. camel
4. tiger
5. giraffe
6. cockroach
7. spider

H5

1. as
2. than
3. more
4. more
5. than
6. as
7. as
8. prettier
9. better
10. as easy
11. better
12. more common
13. nicer

H6

Last year most of the students **signed up** for a trip to Yellowstone National Park. They **carried** their sleeping bags.

Eight popular teachers **accompanied** the students. The principal **stayed** at school. Some parents **joined** the group in order to help the teachers.

Before leaving for Yellowstone Park, one of the teachers **advised** the students to be careful with the wild animals. Especially he **mentioned** scorpions, bears, snakes and wolves.

He also **talked** about the dangers of straying away from the group. **He did not mean** to frighten the students. Luckily **there were** no lions, and tigers at the park.